COVERED
BY
HIS GRACE

ANGELA PEDIGO

WESTBOW
PRESS®
A DIVISION OF THOMAS NELSON
& ZONDERVAN

WestBow Press books may be ordered through booksellers or by contacting:

WestBow Press
A Division of Thomas Nelson & Zondervan
1663 Liberty Drive
Bloomington, IN 47403
www.westbowpress.com
844-714-3454

ISBN: 979-8-3850-0256-6 (sc)
ISBN: 979-8-3850-0255-9 (hc)
ISBN: 979-8-3850-0257-3 (e)

Library of Congress Control Number: 2023912917

Print information available on the last page.

WestBow Press rev. date: 07/20/2023

Dedicated to Jesus Christ, my Savior, my Redeemer.

CONTENTS

INTRODUCTION

I believe God grooms and chisels us to serve a purpose. Once we are living that purpose, we can look back and see His hand throughout the course of our lives actually preparing us for that very thing He has called us to do. Sometimes it's a matter of getting our pride out of the way, ending our denial, or just being willing to forgive ourselves after God forgives us. If we allow others to see our victories, we should allow them to see our brokenness where God's grace met our mistakes.

I pray that as you absorb the lessons in this book and reflect on your own path, you find where God's hand has been over your life. I pray God reveals the work He has for you to do, whether it is by using your past or in spite of it.

The events of your life do not have to set limits on your walk with God. We place limits on ourselves when we give way to those feelings of failure, regret, shame, guilt, and unworthiness. If God is calling you to work for Him in any capacity, He qualifies you to do so as the person you are, and He will continue to grow you in the days to follow. We don't have to understand it or question it. He doesn't expect us to be perfect *before* He uses us for His purpose. We just have to be willing. Trust in Him. Have faith in His leading direction. Embrace the love He has for you through the eyes of our marvelous Creator. His love has no limits.

CHAPTER 1

SO IT BEGINS

I was born to the father and mother I needed, parents who would groom and mold me for experiences that lie ahead. They were great parents, not perfect parents. They were mine, and I love them very much. I learned so much from them, whether it was what to do or not to do. But as a child, I could not see the value of my raising. And the manner in which they lived their lives wouldn't always be the manner in which I would live mine.

My mother is the most biblical definition of how God made a woman to love, serve, and worship Him, her husband, her children, and her neighbors. She has been an example of the true "Proverbs wife." I can honestly say I have never once witnessed her say one mean or cross word to anyone, even when she had what seemed like every justifiable reason to do so. She is kind, compassionate, loving, and caring. She reaches out to the poor and the sick and visits the widows and elderly. She took care of her parents throughout their failing health unlike anyone I've ever seen.

After her parents and my father passed, she began

ministering weekly to residents in five different nursing homes in the surrounding area, no matter if they were old friends, acquaintances, or strangers. She found residents who seem to have no family to visit them, and she "adopted" them as her way of service. She checked on them once a week, bringing them newspapers and treats and seeing after their needs.

Growing up, she took me to church three times a week and any additional time the doors were open, not for show or status but to learn about Jesus. She believed it was her duty to God and to her children. This went on until I was old enough to make the decision for myself as to how devoted I wanted to be with church attendance.

There were times I would get quite frustrated about going to church as a young teenager, but she never failed to let me know it wasn't an option. I plainly remember a time on a Wednesday night in middle school when I had a great deal of history homework due the next day. She still wouldn't let me stay home. I had to take my history book, sit in the back row, and do my homework while the service was going on. You may be thinking, *What good did that do?* It sent a clear message to me: there were no excuses. On the ride to church, I felt like this was ridiculous because I wouldn't even know what the preacher was saying. Obviously, I would be doing homework. I definitely had that teenager attitude of wanting to do what I wanted to, and of course, I knew everything, or so I thought. But when the service started, I found myself not doing my homework but listening to the preacher. When I got home, I completed my homework with ease. I got something out of the preacher's message and my mother's message: "When your priorities are aligned to put God first, He will equip you to do the things you need to." It's funny how I remember to this day the message she sent, but I can't for the life of me remember the preacher's message. I do remember it was interesting, and I was glad I went. But sometimes the most profound messages are the messages parents send to their kids that don't come in lecture form.

My father, although not attending church with us up to this point, insisted I go. He was a "do as I say, not as I do" man for many years. He believed in God and loved Jesus, but golf had his heart. He never missed a chance to play golf on Saturday and Sunday, nor on many evenings when he got home from work. Golf was his priority for approximately twenty to twenty-five years. I can't imagine how many prayers my mom must have prayed for him to form a relationship with Jesus. I don't know how she endured many of those years raising my sister and me basically alone, with never a cross word about doing so. She just stayed the course. To many, this may appear weak, as if she were a classic doormat. I wondered why she would never stand up to him and the temper he often displayed. It did not, however, mean she was weak. She was actually exhibiting unimaginable strength, fighting back by being still and praying.

Where did her strength come from? How did she exhibit that level of patience for so long? I wonder if she ever felt like God was not listening to her prayers. How many times was she tempted to give up on my dad yet never did? She has the strongest faith of anyone I've ever known, a faith that is patient and longsuffering.

In Sunday school class each week, I learned all the amazing

stories of the Bible and the miracles God performed. I had never witnessed a real-life miracle from what my childlike mind could tell, so the stories seemed like a great cartoon to me as a child.

Growing up, on a rare occasion, I would find Daddy missing from his usual spots of being in front of the television or swinging a golf club to fine-tune his swing. I would wander through the house looking for him, and much to my surprise, I would find him lying on his bed reading his Bible. It's the only book I ever saw him read my whole life. It sure must have been an important book. How could he care about the Bible when he did not even go to church? I would quietly walk away when I found him with his Bible. I don't know if he ever knew I was there or not. Even at seven or eight years old, I knew enough to know that I did not want him to stop reading it.

The pastor of our church left after being there for what felt like forever to me; he was the only pastor we'd had for as long as I could remember. We had a new pastor sent to us from out of state. His name was Pastor Dave. He was closer to my sister's age, and surprisingly, he loved playing golf. He asked some of the church members if there were any local golf courses in the area and if any of them played golf. They told him about my dad, who was the club champion for several years at our local country club. Pastor Dave reached out to Daddy in the days to come to introduce himself and ask if he would play golf with him. Daddy was honored, and of course, he was not going to turn down a chance to play. Who would have thought that the beginning of Daddy's developing relationship with Jesus would begin on the golf course? A friendship grew between Daddy and Pastor Dave, and they became so close that I believe Daddy may have felt as if Pastor Dave was the son he never had.

Pastor Dave and his wife had two small girls whom I often babysat. They spent a lot of time at our house, and my parents became like substitute grandparents for the girls since their families did not live close by. Thus, the bond continued to grow to the point that Daddy decided he would go to church to hear Pastor Dave preach. The decision to go was out of support for his friend, in his mind, more so than the thought of needing to hear more about God. At first, I expected this to be a "one and done" thing, but Daddy began to develop more friendships with the church members who had mostly been acquaintances up to this point.

He began to see a new way of life and adopt different priorities; the exciting life he'd thought he'd been living no longer held the same appeal. He began to develop a new kind of love for people. All these things began to work on him, pulling him away from his love for golf. His eyes were opening to see clearly his surroundings, both inwardly and outwardly. And these new friendships were growing deeper with love and admiration. He had no idea what he had been missing, honestly.

The relationship that began to mean the most to Daddy was his relationship with God. Looking back, God's timing was perfect. I was beginning to enter into a rebellious phase as a teenager. I remember saying to Mom that if Daddy did not have to go to church, I shouldn't have to either. But God stopped that argument. He brought Daddy to church. I then stopped hating to go. I wanted to be in church with him. This was new to me: to have one of my heroes improving his own life. To watch this perfectly imperfect man, whom I held in high regard, making a conscious effort to begin living a Christian life—well, there are no words for how that makes a daughter feel. This was not your "parting the Red Sea" kind of miracle. This was a miracle of breaking Daddy's will, transforming him by using someone He sent to our church and, surprisingly, removing the love of the thing Daddy always put before God by using the very thing Daddy put before God. When I say "God is in the details," He truly is! Who else uses golf to break a love of golf besides God?

You can fill in the blank with your own top priority. Now, being completely honest with yourself, what has been standing between you and God? Could God be trying to use that very thing to get you to a place where you allow Him to be your priority instead? If you notice that you do not enjoy something you once did, look for where God may be at work in that situation. He may be pulling you away from it because He has something better for you. And because you can't see it or may not want to fathom it not holding that place in your life anymore, whether it's someone or something, you may be losing joy and the blessings He has in store for you because you aren't surrendering it to God.

These transformations are often so gradual that we fail to look at the details in them. It took time for this chiseling process to occur in Daddy, but it was miraculous nonetheless. I never saw it as a miracle until the last few years.

Lessons come in all shapes and sizes. One of the lessons I learned early in life was actually taught to me by my sister.

She is older than me, and I always looked up to her. She has always tried to help me succeed, no matter if it was a contest, sports, school, work, faith, life, etc. She is such an amazing big sister! We are quite different in many ways, but we love each other immensely.

When I was a kid, there was a kids' contest at church to raise money for the alabaster offering our church participated in each year. This offering raised funds for building other churches. The boy and girl who raised the most money would be announced in a few weeks as the alabaster king and queen. As the weeks went on, my sister coached me to not tell anyone how much money I had raised. She said, "Just be quiet. Don't brag about it because others will want to know how much you have raised so that they can raise more at the last minute." No one really asked that often about how much I had raised until the last day. This one girl tried so hard to get an amount out of me, but I didn't answer. I sat calmly, trying not to care who won even though the excitement was building within. When the program began, at the point the announcer was about to name the winners, we all sat on the edge of our seats in anticipation.

"And the winner is ... Angie," came across the microphone. I got up, went up front, and accepted the prize, which happened to be a crown like that of a queen. I couldn't believe it! I honestly didn't expect to really get a great prize like a crown, but it was very exciting to my little mind.

My sister said, "Whatever you do, do not brag about it." So I stayed quiet and kept to myself. You may be thinking this is just kids being kids, right? Yes, it was, but the lesson my sister taught me I have never forgotten: whether in sports, in relationships, or in work situations. That message was to walk humbly, not to brag, and be thankful.

A few years later, Pastor Dave managed to talk me into going to a weeklong church camp. At twelve years old, I had never been away from home before without my parents. I didn't know if I could actually do it. Two of my friends were also going, but they were two years older than me. They were in a different age group, leaving me with younger kids I didn't know. I decided to go anyway after much persuasion. I am so thankful I did because that decision changed my life forever.

There were a lot of fun things to do at camp: meeting new people, which by the way I had no idea up until that week just how much I enjoyed getting to know strangers; singing, which was always a hobby of mine from the time I was three; playing games; shaving cream fights; and best of all, amazing worship services with kids my age. These services left me with such anticipation for the next service, just to see what was in store.

Back home at church, I tended to hold every emotion and feeling inside, afraid if I cried, my parents would think I had done something wrong and I could get in trouble later. Besides that, I had enough pride to not want anyone to see me cry. Camp was different, though. Being in a setting with kids my age and seeing how they allowed themselves to publicly show emotion and freely worship made me realize I was missing something. I was apparently craving this freedom in my soul. Those walls I had up began to be torn down at a rapid pace from watching the others worship with such freedom and joy.

The services were held at an outdoor pavilion. One night, after the preacher was finished with the message, there was an altar call. Something was stirring inside my heart. The Holy Spirit was dealing with me heavily. As the tears started falling uncontrollably, I realized I was not fighting back like normal. I was letting go, allowing myself to feel. I was allowing the Holy Spirit to come closer, to move inside my heart. Could it be that this wall may finally be torn down?

As I looked around, I saw other kids my age crying happy tears, lifting their hands up to praise and worship God. I was just so shocked that kids my age actually did that. That night, I laid down my pride. I made my move up to that altar. Some lady was up there talking to me, and all I can remember her saying was, "Tell Him everything." I began praying, pouring my heart out to God, confessing all the sins in my life, and begging for Him to forgive me and take them away, to save me. I didn't want to die, but the thought of being left behind scared me so much. I feared Jesus's return and my family and friends being gone and me being left behind.

There was a moment in time I can't fully explain. It was like a blank space in time. It seemed as though my heart was communicating with Jesus directly. It felt like it went on for twenty minutes, but it may very well have been more like two or three minutes. I have no idea honestly. All I know is that it was just Jesus and me. I was seeking forgiveness and grace. I prayed for the relationship with Him that I saw others have. I wanted to walk with Him every day of my life going forward. And then it happened! He saved me. He saved my soul. He washed all of my sins away. It was like Jesus cleaned out all the darkness and placed light in my heart and a kind of peace so completely unexplainable. I got up from that altar, went back to my seat, and began to worship with the others. He had literally just saved me!

At the time, there was a war going on in the Middle East. Before that night at camp, I could hardly listen to the news when my parents watched it each evening because it tormented me. I just knew there was a bomb out there with my name on it waiting to blow me up and I wasn't ready to die. I knew I did not have Jesus in my heart. I could feel something was missing, like a separation or an isolation kind of feeling. But that night when the service was over at camp when I received grace, the minute I stepped off that concrete pad onto the grass out from under the roof of the pavilion, I felt like I was walking on air. I distinctly remember looking up at the sky and saying, "Hit me now. I dare you." What relief! I knew I wasn't going to be left behind now.

One of the reasons I had delayed seeking Jesus up to this point was because I did not want to be questioned about what was wrong with me or if I had done something wrong. Going to camp placed me in an environment where the only thing to share when I returned was the gift of salvation I received there although I didn't share it with anyone, really, when I got back. I honestly didn't know how to talk about what I had experienced yet.

Communication was not easy in our home. Daddy did the talking. We did the listening and spoke very few words back to him. Back talking or questioning anything he would say or think was considered disrespectful and would not be tolerated. I would shut down and stay out of sight a lot as a kid when Daddy was around for that reason. I spent a great deal of time with friends. I would open up to my friends about almost anything, but never at home. I'm certain I took my frustrations out on my mom because she was my outlet to say everything I couldn't say to him in anger. It wasn't always pretty. I should never have talked to her the way I did with the anger I felt inside. She certainly didn't deserve it, but she understood it. She gave me more grace than I deserved for sure. It was that same grace I used to question why she showed my dad, not seeing I needed it as much as he did.

It is so important to give your children a voice, allowing them to be heard. This by no means indicates you should give them everything they want. It means allowing them to learn the art of communication first with you so that they know how to communicate with others and, more importantly, with God. It is a foundational building block for your children to feel free to approach you when they need to the most. Giving your children a voice simply means that you allow them the space to be genuinely heard without judgment or belittlement. Then you may use it as a teachable moment, explaining the real reason why you ask the questions you ask, give the answers you give, and make the decisions you do.

One of the most impactful things Daddy ever told me was no when I couldn't do something or have something I wanted. Once, I got up the courage to ask him why I couldn't go spend the night at a friend's house. There seemed to be no logical reason for me not to get to go. It wasn't like we had plans to be somewhere, and I was just getting frustrated at being told no more than usual it seemed. So mustering up enough courage in my frustration, I asked, "Why not?" It was a rare moment for me to challenge him this way. Rather than yell at me for questioning him, which I did not expect, he used that moment to teach me one of the most valuable lessons of my life.

"You are going to learn the value of the word *no* because in this life, you are not going to get everything you want. And you need to know how to handle that." What wisdom! The kid in me didn't like it, but it was a seed planted deep within me that has been an anchor in my life even to this day.

When camp was over and I was back home, I began to read my Bible like I had seen my parents do. I was determined to read through it from start to finish, wanting to know everything possible about God and being a Christian. I read daily devotionals too. I wouldn't ask my parents or church members any questions I might have along the way, though. I was too embarrassed to do so, and these were things we just didn't talk about with one another. I just took away what interpretations I could from it each day, along with what I would hear at church being taught and preached. My mom bought me a teen Bible that was easy to understand, which helped a great deal.

I began to love the history of the Bible. Seeing the stories in chronological order made them more real. The maps in the back of the Bible brought the stories to life. It put a location on the events I was reading about and the stories I had been taught in Sunday school. They became less mythical and more realistic. Little did I know, this too was further preparation for the future.

CHAPTER 2

NEEDING A GUIDE

At age fifteen, this guy, who was two years older than me, began to pay attention to me at a pep rally one day. He had that flirtatious way about him that would attract girls. I even remember the cologne he wore being another lure. We got to know each other by talking between classes.

During homecoming week, my friends and I were gearing up for the homecoming dance. I didn't have a date to the dance, but it was fine because my friends and I were planning to have a good time. After all, this was my first high school dance, which came with nerves, excitement, and plans to stand against a wall and lie low.

Once we got there and the music was playing, people began to dance. Much to my surprise, this same guy asked me to dance ... twice! I was completely swept off my feet! We became a "thing" in the days to follow. This "thing," however, lasted about four months and was filled with excitement and thrills and finally became empty and broken.

He was a free spirit, which was such an added layer of attraction. He wore an earring, which I knew my dad would hate if he found out. I couldn't officially go out on a date until I was sixteen, and that was nine months away. His fun didn't slow down though, being as he was older than me. In the evenings while I was home, he would hang out with his friends in town where most teenagers would gather together. I trusted him, being I was so young and naïve. I didn't have a reason not to.

I began pulling away from my closest friends to hang out with his crowd while at school. Fortunately, some of my friends from elementary school were doing the same thing, hanging with this older crowd, but their parents were not as strict as mine. They were allowed to date at fifteen years old. I was trying to fit into a place I wasn't used to, and it was awkward, to say the least. Being naive also proved to be another weakness in this situation. What I didn't know was that in my absence in the evenings, he was growing close to someone else.

I began compromising my morals and values to fit in, thinking I needed to in order to keep him. I changed the music I listened to, took my first drink of alcohol one night while spending the night with some friends, and would sneak around to see him. Struggling and in the middle of an identity crisis, I couldn't talk to my friends about it, partly because I felt like they didn't understand and the other part being that I believed they would disown me, judge me, and also be upset that I had walked away from most of them to chase him and his friends. To be honest, I felt ashamed to talk to them. I could not whatsoever talk to my parents for obvious reasons. We did not have an open-communication kind of relationship. To talk to them would have meant consequences to come. So I sat in this space, feeling stuck, not wanting out, but wanting out at the same time and not knowing how to get out. I wanted to go back to the life I had before changing myself for someone else.

For your children to come to you with the highs and lows of life, it takes more than just telling them they can. It requires building trust with them. Trust comes from not sharing the things they open up about with others, not screaming or yelling at them when they ask for advice or guidance. It requires listening more and talking less when they open up about their broken heart with you. It is about helping them think through things in a safe space, letting them know the consequences they face without insulting or degrading them. Your words as parents should always leave your children better than they were, not torn down because you feel angry or embarrassed by their choices.

You will never be successful at shaming your children into doing the right thing. There will never be anything you can say to break someone down, who is already down, to the point they open their eyes. Your words will only validate what they already think about themselves. You never know what someone is dealing with inside, and that includes your children.

The parable of the lost sheep in Matthew 18:10–14 explains if a man has one hundred sheep and one of them goes astray, he leaves the ninety-nine to go after the one. When he finds the one, he rejoices over it. I encourage you to read this passage of scripture because nowhere in the text does it mention the man was angry, yelled, slurred, or insulted the one for going astray in the first place. The man sought to go help restore the one.

It takes a great deal of self-control to tame anger and fear over your children and their choices many times. But self-control is not something you have to do alone. Self-control is a fruit of the Holy Spirit. If you know Jesus as your Lord and Savior, the Holy Spirit lives inside of you and supplies all the self-control you need in any situation. You just have to ask for it, especially at that moment. Sometimes your children need a coach, and that requires self-control as their parent to respond rather than react.

God sent someone to come looking for me, the one who was lost. My basketball coach, whom I loved dearly, called me into his office one day on my lunch break at school. As I sat across the desk from him, he asked how I was doing. I told him I was good, pretending to be OK. Then he said the words that began to make me feel safe and able to talk. He said, "You know I love you like one of my daughters, right? And I see you hurting." Suddenly, all of that emotion and fear I had been holding in came pouring out.

Coach was a gentle soul. He was kind and loved us all like family. For the first time maybe ever, I felt like I had found a safe place to open up and talk to someone with honesty and without repercussions. My walls began to come down, pouring out my heart in confidence to him about what my struggles were with myself. He listened so intently. That day, he actually cried with me because he was truly hurting for me. It was like a father's love that I needed so badly. It was like the love I suppose God our Father has for us. Coach wasn't there to judge me. He truly wanted to guide me out of this space I was in. And all it took was a few sentences. He simply said, "When he walks in those doors each day entering this school, he lives in your world. When he walks out of those doors at the end of the day, he lives in his world. And you are not a part of that world." *Wow.* What a reality check! What a wake-up call. He said it with such care and kindness, not in a way to tell me what to do, but just helping me to understand and put things in perspective. It was up to me what I would do with this wisdom he just spoke. I walked away from this conversation knowing what I had to do, and I even had relief over my decision.

Coach wasn't being judgmental of me or of my boyfriend. He was merely saying we were different. We were in two different places. I couldn't date. He could. He didn't want to sit at home and wait on me. We had different friends, his being older and more mature. Not that one is better than the other, just different. And it was time to stop trying to be someone I wasn't at that point in my life.

In the weeks ahead, I pondered what Coach said to me, and he was right. I could see it more and more. We broke up after school was out about two weeks later, which was for the best because we couldn't see each other all summer.

So what's the point of sharing this moment in my life? The point is that open communication with your children, no matter the subject matter, is crucial. Many children, no matter their age, long to come to their parents with their problems, not to strangers or even friends really, nor left to figure it out for themselves when they aren't mature enough to know how. Love and understanding can cover a multitude of hurts, traumas, and mistakes, preventing scars your children could potentially carry for the rest of their lives.

Coach became a life coach for me at that moment. Now,

just imagine if we all coached our children rather than yelling, ignoring or dismissing them, or creating such a perfectionist environment around them, that to admit anything less is considered unacceptable. Our kids need us to be real. They need us to be human, not full of so much pride that we only acknowledge their accomplishments but not their struggles. They need us to be present, which requires in this day and time putting down electronic devices and muting the noise, giving our undivided attention for a time. You can be present for your children physically every day of their lives, buy them anything they want, and take care of supplying their basic needs, but if you are emotionally absent, you risk creating a breeding ground for codependence within them.

School started back in August. About six weeks before my sixteenth birthday, a very popular guy in school asked me to the football homecoming dance. I was surprised that he would even look my way, not to mention ask me to the dance. He was tall, handsome, and a star athlete.

In the days to follow after the dance, I was concerned that he wouldn't wait on me to be old enough to actually date him. Daddy was adamant that I would not date until I was at least sixteen years old, which was six weeks away. We did, however, get to see each other quite often because I also played sports in high school just like he did. We saw each other at games, during school, and at practices after school.

When my ex-boyfriend found out I was dating someone new, he wanted to get back together. There were parts of me that wanted to rekindle that relationship despite how different we were. So what made me think this time would be any better? Well, I was sixteen at this point and could date, and he knew that. I really had to take a step back from both of them and ask God what to do here. My mind was saying to stay in this new relationship. My emotions were saying give my ex another chance. What I didn't realize at the time was that I was actually praying for discernment and wisdom, not calling it that because I didn't know what those things were. But that is what was happening looking back on it.

The Holy Spirit provides gifts of discernment and wisdom to navigate us through this life, and we can ask for this help through prayer. Discernment is the ability to see a situation clearly for what it is, discerning what is right and what is wrong about it. Wisdom is knowing how to apply knowledge about a situation to make the best choice or decision.

Do you find it difficult to ask God for direction over areas of your life, such as relationships, jobs/careers, children, etc.? Is it because you want to remain in control, fearful that God may not work things out the way you want Him to? Maybe it's because you want what you want, even if it's wrong or harmful to yourself or others. Do you feel selfish if you ask God to help you personally, but have no problem asking Him to help others? Sometimes you may not ask God for guidance or help because you may find it hard to trust that He will answer, and if you don't ask, then you won't be let down. Let's address each of these schools of thought.

The feeling of being in control may run deep for you as a way to achieve the outcome you desire. You may not allow God to be in control of situations in your life because He might not bring about your desired outcome. But He may not be willing to let you have it your way because He may know that your way is not what you need and could hurt you or pull you away from a relationship with Him.

Do you see God as a parent telling you not to jump off a chair because you could get hurt, but you want to jump anyway? To untangle this false belief, paint this picture in your mind: God isn't there to only tell you not to jump. He is there to say, "Don't jump from here or you will fall and get hurt. So let me pick you up and place you over there so that when you jump, you can fly." If you aren't willing to let God into those decisions to guide you, you may very well forfeit a blessing for your life.

Sometimes people are willing to accept the fall just to get what they want or what they think they need. A desire for control of an outcome causes people to act out of a lack of self-control. We need to be able to tell ourselves no just as much as we need to be able to tell others no. When people follow emotions (what *feels* good) rather than direction (what *is* good), they tend to find themselves in worse positions.

We as human beings tend to go back to what is familiar to us. Even if it is an unhealthy situation and knowing it isn't where God wants us, we will go back to the pit we just came from because we know what to expect there. Sometimes that pit is what we feel we deserve as a means of self-punishment when we live with shame and guilt from our pasts. None of this is where God would have us to remain. His word tells us in John 10:10 (NAS95), "The thief comes only to steal and kill and destroy; I came that they may have life, and have it abundantly."

You may feel selfish or greedy when asking God to help you in times of trouble. This couldn't be farther from the truth, and the Bible confirms this. For example, in many of the encounters Jesus had with those He saved and healed, He would ask, "What do you want Me to do for you?" just as He did in Matthew 20:32 (NAS95) when He addressed the two blind men. If it was wrong to ask Jesus for help, He certainly would not have tempted anyone to be selfish by asking the question in the first place. But as long as Satan continues whispering that lie in your ear to the point you believe it, he prevents miracles from happening over your life. The Bible tells us in Matthew 7:7 (NAS95): "Ask, and it will be given to you; seek, and you will find; knock, and it will be opened to you." The stories in the Bible, whether Old Testament stories of cries for deliverance from an army or evil king to stories in the New Testament for gifts of healing, each answer came by making a request known to God. There is no need to feel selfish by asking God for help. He wants us to rely on Him. When the Israelites in Exodus 16 were wandering in the wilderness headed for the promised land, God took care of them by raining down manna from heaven each morning to feed them. They were instructed to only gather a day's worth and to consume it that day, not keeping any leftovers. Any left each day would rot overnight. But on the sixth day, they would gather enough for two days because they were not allowed to gather on the Sabbath. If God could rain down enough for two days, why not rain enough down once a week? He could have kept it from rotting and worms forming in the leftovers. But collecting manna daily served more of a purpose than nutrition. This daily gift of sustenance taught them to rely on God *daily* to survive. God wants the same for us: daily renewed dependence on Him for all the big and small things in our lives.

Another reason to bring your requests to God about yourself is that you may be the only person who knows the problem you face. If no one is praying for your specific need because they don't know to, how else will you take that need before God's throne unless you ask? Some people argue the point that the Bible teaches us that God already knows what we need before we even ask. Yes, He knows, but James 4:2 (NAS95) also teaches us that "we have not because we ask not." First Peter 5:6–7 (NAS95) says this, "Therefore humble yourselves under the mighty hand of God, that He may exalt you at the proper time, casting all your anxiety on Him, because He cares for you." If you care about it, God wants to hear it.

Now, if you are someone who does not ask God for specific help because of doubt, do you believe He *can't* or that He *won't* do it for you? Be honest with yourself and really think about that question. You first have to believe He can before you will begin to believe that He will do it for you.

Do you believe you have to first obtain a monumental level of faith before God will answer your prayers? I used to think this way myself. Let's untwist that lie as well. The Bible tells us in Matthew 17:20 that the faith of a mustard seed can move a mountain: a literal mountain! What mountains are you not seeing move simply because you won't ask?

There is a story in Mark 9 where a father of a boy possessed with an unclean spirit came to Jesus asking if He can heal his son. Jesus said to the boy's father that all things are possible for those that believe. Verse 24 says, "Immediately the boy's

father cried out and said, 'I do believe; help my unbelief.'"
I can just imagine how that conversation would have gone
down in today's terms: "I have *one* mustard seed, Jesus! *One*
seed of faith. Please use this one seed to heal my boy and
use it to grow my faith more! It's all I have. One!" What
a blessing it is that one mustard seed–size amount is all it
takes to witness miracles! The more you invite God into
your life by seeking His direction, intervention, strength,
healing, etc., the more of a platform you give Him to grow
your faith. The more you see God work and move in your
life, that mustard seed gets planted, watered, and grows into
a strong tree of faith.

This does not mean that He will always answer the
way you want Him to. Faith can still grow by trusting that
because He didn't answer the way you wanted, He obviously
knows something you don't or has a plan you may not see.
It is choosing to trust that He does all things for your good
as evidenced in Romans 8:28 (NAS95), "And we know that
God causes all things to work together for good to those who
love God, to those who are called according to His purpose."

When you are tempted to take matters into your own
hands and lean on your own understanding in a situation, you
risk falling victim to your emotions. Emotions can lead you
wrong. A great deal of my life was spent being emotionally
driven, but when I began to think logically rather than react
emotionally, I saw how little I had figured out about myself
or anything else for that matter. I needed guidance from the
only One who knew me fully, and that was God.

Dating in my teenage years was supremely difficult. The
rules my dad had were next to impossible while trying to

keep a boyfriend. I was caught between the two in what felt like a game of tug-of-war, neither of which seemed to care about how it was affecting me, but caring about who was winning the war. I was trying to keep both sides happy so I didn't lose the guy or get in trouble with my dad. Daddy had rules that went beyond curfew. I could only see my boyfriend two nights a week. My boyfriend had to pick me up, even if my car would run and his was broken down. He would have to borrow a car to come get me. I had to be home at a certain time, and if I asked for the rules to be changed, it did not go well. If my boyfriend came over to our house, it was most uncomfortable. Daddy had this edge about him that said without saying, "I've got my eyes on you, boy." Needless to say, dates were spent elsewhere, either going out or going to his house.

I dated this one boy for a couple of years, and we were growing increasingly weary of the two-nights-per-week rule among others. So by October of my senior year, we became engaged. I was so excited that I didn't even consider how I was going to break the news to my parents. I was only seventeen years old. What was I thinking? I loved him, and getting married may solve the problem of being so torn all the time trying to keep them both happy. I needed peace and thought I would find it in marriage.

When I got up the next morning after he proposed, I went into the kitchen to show my mom my engagement ring. She just smiled and said, "Now go tell your dad." It felt like the longest walk down that hallway. Daddy was still in bed. I tiptoed in there and sat on the bed. I just stuck my hand out. When he saw the ring, he immediately covered up his head with his blankets. He tried to be happy for me, but I could tell he was so disheartened. I tried soothing his mind by telling him it would be a long engagement. I don't know if that helped or not, but we never really talked about it anymore.

Now that I was engaged, I thought the two-nights-per-week rule would be removed and we could take our time. But it remained in force. Daddy was not going to bend an inch. I don't know if it was out of pride or out of hoping he could stop this relationship or both. Either way, I couldn't deal with it anymore. That's when the wedding date quickly got moved up. We planned our wedding to be in October of the next year, just five months after I graduated high school.

I was offered a work-study scholarship to a nearby community college, which I turned down because I now had to work a full-time job. I could only attend college part-time. I chose this long, hard road trying to fix a short-term problem. It took me the next five years to get an associate's degree at that pace.

I often think of what some give-and-take and communication might have changed in that time of my life. If I could have been allowed to speak without consequence, would it have changed anything? If I had a safe space to share what was so difficult, not to get my way but to find common ground, could we have all grown together? Could we have set pride aside and been able to compromise? If I could have opened up and shared that I wasn't ready to get married, but I just needed this tug-of-war to end, could Daddy have helped me through that by giving a little? Could we have been allies rather than enemies?

I also wonder if I had gone to college on that scholarship rather than getting married, would I have finished in two years rather than five? Would we have married or not, or would I have gone on to finish my degree? Or would we have married when we were more mature to handle it? It would have given us time to see who we were and if who we were together was something that had forever qualities.

People need a voice, an opportunity to be heard without criticism and chastisement. In the case of your children, it does not mean to give them everything they want, nor does it mean you should agree with everything they say or do but a voice that says, "I hear you." Creating a safe space for young adults to gain wisdom in a loving, nurturing environment is invaluable. Coaching them is not spoiling them or enabling them. It is being a coach, a mentor, and a guide. Coaching your children helps build trust between the two of you. Coaching isn't a stream of demands. It is listening and guiding to solve problems and build trust. Coaching involves listening and then guiding them to arrive at their own realizations, laying out the choices before them with the pros and cons of each one, and allowing them to feel that their thoughts matter, even if the decision is still your decision as a parent to make in the end.

Let me make this known here. My dad was a good father. He parented the way he did because he loved us, not to be mean to us. He wanted to protect us, expected the best out of us, and made sure he prepared us to handle life. He taught me many lessons, sometimes from his wisdom and sometimes through his mistakes. I could ask the "what if" questions over and over, but at the end of the day, it will not change the past. The past, however, can be used to change the future for me, my son, and others who may find themselves in these similar places, either as a teen or a young adult struggling to choose a path or as a parent trying to maintain a relationship with one's teenagers.

The moral of the story is not to rush into a long-term decision to fix a short-term problem. Pray and seek God's will, asking for patience when yours seems to be running out. Examine all of your avenues and the pros and cons of each rather than following your emotions to solutions you are not necessarily prepared to endure.

CHAPTER 3

LIFE'S LESSONS

I had an idea of what married life would be like. It would be a warm, cozy, loving feeling of togetherness and companionship. Oh, how naïve I was. Marriage was much harder and looked way different than I envisioned.

I grew up believing that even though I was saved by grace if I had any sin in my life and died before repenting of it, I would spend eternity in hell. I lived in constant worry, knowing that I could not live perfectly enough to get into heaven. Now, as a wife, I tried to model my role after my mother, who was as close to perfection as anyone I had ever known. But the more I tried to live perfectly, the deeper a wedge grew between my husband and me. No one can live free when living in fear, and I was projecting that onto him by default. My reason for trying to live so close to God was way different than that of my mother's reasons. My reason was that I thought God expected us to be perfect once we become saved by His grace, and anything shy of that somehow made my salvation null and void. My mother, however, obeyed God out of the immense love she had for Him. It's the difference between wanting to and having to. I felt an expectation to "be perfect" driven by fear, therefore setting myself up for failure. I also placed that expectation onto my marriage as a whole, that it should be as perfect as possible; and well, that just was not the case.

Unreasonable expectations set the stage for failure from the start. Whether it is an expectation you have placed on yourself or others, it does not generally end well. When you place unreasonable expectations on yourself and fail to meet them, a whirlwind of self-bashing occurs over feeling guilty, shameful, and eventually failure. You can become trapped in this cycle, therefore stunting growth in your life and your walk with God. If you sit in this headspace long enough, you risk letting this self-imposed shame drag you down so low that you may feel hopeless and helpless.

Forgiving yourself can be hard. When Jesus forgives your sins, He is doing just that—extending grace to you. You are going to make mistakes because no one is a perfect being. The Bible tells us in Romans 3:23 (NAS95), "For all have sinned and fall short of the glory of God." It becomes a matter of whether or not you seek forgiveness for those things or if you hold on to them until they rob you of joy in your life. If Jesus can give you grace, you certainly should be able to give yourself grace. Grace is your defense against the bully in your mind trying to imprison you in your thoughts and emotions. Are your judgments higher than those of your Savior? Not even close. Why, then, once Jesus forgives you do you say, "Thanks, Jesus, but I just can't forgive myself"? See, the enemy wants you to harbor unforgiveness in your heart any way he can convince you to do so, even if it is toward yourself. It keeps you bound and imprisoned by your own shackles until your heart becomes hardened and hopeless. The enemy's goal is to get you to the point of giving up so that you won't rise up in the strength of the Holy Spirit and potentially impact the lives of others with your testimony.

You may choose to not forgive yourself because you have held that shame and guilt for so long you don't know who you are without it, dragging it into every relationship you've had in your life, including your relationship with God. The very thought of living truly free can be scary when it isn't a state of being that is familiar to you. Fear of the unknown causes many people to hold shame and guilt far too long. If this is you, I challenge you to let go and find out! Forgiveness is where true healing begins, whether it is forgiveness from God, self, or others.

Now, you are not going to just respond to that challenge with an "OK, I'll forgive me." It takes a lot of work to surrender unforgiveness. Why specifically are you holding resentment toward yourself? After answering that question, ask yourself if the resentment is actually valid or based on a lie. It amazes me how quickly we can come to an agreement with the lies in our minds about ourselves. The best test to this is to take each individual thought you have toward yourself captive to the throne of God to test its validity. Is the thought what God would say about you? After all, He created you with a plan and purpose in mind. He does not make junk. He didn't have a creative oops when he made you. If your thoughts do not come into agreement with His thoughts and words toward you, then you are most likely harboring unforgiveness toward yourself.

Now let's look at the role of expectations in a relationship.

Placing unrealistic expectations on someone means you expect them to be someone they are not or to do something they may have never shown you they can or will do. When they do not meet your expectation, you may become disappointed, angry, or hurt, which all lead to resentment if left unchecked.

Expectations are a large part of many relationship struggles. Many people want what they want and tend to not show much grace when their expectations are not met. We as a society have forgotten how to allow people to be themselves. This does not mean you should compromise your personal beliefs, morals, or values. Nor does it mean to accept things contrary to your beliefs. It simply means you should leave the judging between God and them, just like we want others to do for us. Often people are acting out of hurt places that have never healed or traumas they experienced long ago, and they don't know how to heal it. Rather than showing them the love of Jesus, we make it our job to condemn them without ever getting to know where these things stem from. It is not our job to condemn. It's God's role to convict. And there is a difference in conviction and condemnation. God will convict every individual as He sees the need as they grow in their relationship with Him. How are people supposed to want a relationship with Him if they are not shown His love through other believers? We allow unrealistic expectations to divide and conquer relationships between God, others, and ourselves. Unrealistic expectations are therefore effective in separating us from the fruits of the Holy Spirit: "But the fruit of the Spirit is love, joy, peace, patience, kindness, goodness, faithfulness, gentleness, self-control; against such things there is no law" (Galatians 5:22–23 NAS95). Which of these do you lack in your heart because unforgiveness and judgment are taking their place? It is something worth evaluating on a daily basis as new experiences and emotions arise daily.

Some people believe this train of thought is not realistic. After all, how can you go through life without expectations? To understand, let's look at an example. If you have tickets to a concert, you expect the headliner to show up and perform. That is a realistic expectation. There are on occasion concerts that have been canceled for various reasons, therefore it is possible when you purchase that ticket, a realistic expectation knows that something could happen—you could lose this money, or the concert could get postponed to a later date for an unforeseen reason. An unrealistic expectation means you purchased this ticket and expected this concert to happen, regardless of any extenuating circumstances that could occur with the entertainers or the venue. When the concert gets canceled, your anger is raging because your expectation was not met. Unrealistic expectations leave no room for unanticipated factors to be present. And we all know life is going to happen. When life happens, do we give grace or hold resentment?

Let's take this one step further. Have you ever had unrealistic expectations of God? I coach people often that are angry at God. I have been there myself. When God does not meet some expectation we may have had of Him, the question should not be, "Why, God, did you fail me?" The search for understanding should begin within our thoughts surrounding the expectation and what the Word of God says He will in fact do or not do. We can take any verse that says God will do something for us and try to apply it to all of our requests. When He doesn't meet it, we lose faith when actually, there is generally some part of the Word we ignored when we made the request to God. Furthermore, we need to examine what our motives are behind the request. If they came from selfishness or direct disobedience to our Heavenly Father, we should not expect to receive the answer we wanted. He doesn't cosign what He didn't authorize or bless.

My mother's motives to live a Godly life were because she genuinely wanted to out of the love and admiration she has for God, without expectation. I, on the other hand, attempted to live a Godly life from fear-based expectations and therefore placed unrealistic expectations on myself and others. And I couldn't measure up, nor could anyone else meet this measure of perfection. Not realizing this at the time, I kept searching for something, anything, to feel free of this bondage I managed to create in my life.

Not long after I got married, I joined a different church. I felt at home and immediately dove into serving, teaching, and music. I knew God had a job for me to do, and as much as I loved every one of these things, I didn't feel like I had quite stumbled on what that job was just yet.

One day while driving home from work on a country road, I crossed over this rise on the road, where it felt as if God was waiting on me to get there. Everything seemed so bright outside, and the Holy Spirit instructed me in this still small voice to start a youth choir. I felt so much excitement and nervous all at the same time. I loved music so much, but I didn't know where to begin and certainly did not feel worthy or capable to take on such a ministry. We had a lot of youth in our church, but how would I ever get them interested in singing?

Days went by as I pondered over what had been placed on my heart. One Sunday morning before church began, I stopped the youth pastor of the church and shared the direction I had been given on the road that day. Much to my surprise, sheer excitement came over his face. He shared that he and the pastor had been praying for God to send someone to start a youth choir. That was all the affirmation he and I both needed.

The announcement was made, and practices began on the following Wednesday night before service. Three kids came to the first practice. It was awkward at first, but they enjoyed it and began recruiting other kids to join. At the peak of this ministry, there were approximately twenty-four to twenty-six kids regularly in this choir, ranging from third graders up to high school seniors. It was amazing to watch them find an avenue of worship for God. I witnessed them outwardly express their love for God that back when I was their age I couldn't seem to do myself.

These children brought so much comfort to me at a sorrowful time in my life. During this time, I was trying to have a baby, and God was not answering. I felt a lot of anger over the situation, but I kept shoving it down so as to try and stay focused on the children and the youth choir. This went on for over a year and included my taking fertility medication. I was trying to do everything right and live as perfectly as I could, yet God wasn't blessing me with a baby.

I was so hurt, but the problem with this way of thinking was ever believing that God worked on a work/reward system in the first place. God's blessings are gifts of grace, not earned gifts. God not answering my prayers my way for a baby was His way of showing me grace. He knew what was to come, and I was impatient. I wanted a baby to feel loved by someone who might just love me unconditionally, something I had never really felt. Even God's love felt conditional to me based on what I believed about Him.

At the peak of the youth choir, I found myself in the middle of a divorce. We were two completely different people living very different lives. We drifted apart so much that it felt like there was no returning. This was not really a reason to divorce. We were young, having been married nearly five years. We didn't know how to help ourselves through this space we were in now. Because of the divorce, I was asked to resign from my position in the youth choir and teaching the children. It hurt, yet I understood it too. It was embarrassing, to say the least, so I just left the church. I loved that church and the people there so much, but it was just too uncomfortable to stay.

Fast-forwarding to my next relationship, I met a guy where I worked, who lived in the next county over from me. We began dating and eventually got married. I moved to his hometown to live. Our families were close and loved each other very much. We had a great marriage in the beginning. With this move, I began attending church with him some. It was unlike anything I had ever been a part of before. But if it meant as much to him as it did, there had to be something to it.

I spent about a year diving into the Bible again, trying

to learn for the first time what I personally believe. So many religions have different interpretations of the Bible. This being the third religion I had been a part of, I was seeing more and more that there were a lot of varying interpretations of the particulars of Christianity. As I studied, I found clarity on the plan of salvation in the Bible. This was the beginning of a spiritual transformation for me. I began to see God as a loving, caring Father, not a dictator in the sky that liked to smite me each time I made a mistake. As my understanding of God grew, so did my relationship with Him.

The next year, I became pregnant. We were beyond excited! And just as quickly as we found out, days later, I had a miscarriage. It was a difficult and traumatic experience, to say the least. I was so angry, but I eventually chose to trust that God knew best after the way He protected me from my own desires in my first marriage when I was trying so hard to have a child then. I wouldn't allow myself to question why so that I wouldn't feel unnecessary anger toward God.

God saw my pain, and a few months later, I became pregnant again with my son. There are no words to express the emotion I felt. We were so happy, excited, and so nervous all at the same time, especially since my history hadn't been good for pregnancy.

My pregnancy, however, went well. The day our son was born, we experienced so much joy! It was the happiest day of my life, aside from the day Jesus saved my soul. And once again, fear quickly followed the next day. A doctor came into the hospital room with the news that we did not anticipate. He stated that our baby boy needed surgery on his head.

He was born with the two plates in his head already fused together. Without the surgery, his brain couldn't grow.

The surgery was scheduled for when he would turn nine weeks old. The plan was to make an incision from ear to ear across the top of his head and remove a five-centimeter strip of his skull running front to back. This would open his head up so that his brain could grow. This surgery would also require that he have a blood transfusion, which meant we had to find donors to match his blood type or we would have to accept random donors. We had three people volunteer immediately that were matches. I was beyond grateful for them, especially since they were all close family friends.

When we got home from the hospital after he was born and knowing this surgery was coming, all I could do was rock him, sing to him, and pray fervently. When we met with the surgeon days later in his office to go over the procedure, he had to share all the dangers that could happen during surgery. He stated that if he cuts that bone too deep, it could be fatal. There was a main artery running underneath his skull where the cut would be made. If the doctor happened to cut too deep, he would bleed out and not survive the procedure. What a blow! Frightened, I asked the doctor how many of these procedures he had done, which was many. I then asked how many times such a tragedy had ever happened, trying to find any comfort in maybe a very low percentage of tragedies occurring. To this, the doctor shared that it had never happened, but that he wasn't the surgeon. It was just his hands, but God was the surgeon. I immediately felt a wave of peace flood over me, believing in my soul that we had the right doctor. I believed that God would guide his hands to bring my son through this surgery. Leading up to the surgery date, God sustained me with His peace and assurance through Romans 8:28 (NAS95), which states, "And we know that God causes all things to work together for good to those who love God, to those who are the called according to His purpose."

Surgery day came, and the hospital seemed to have the Holy Spirit flowing up and down the halls everywhere we went. Nurses, janitors, and all types of various workers would stop us as we passed in the hall, asking us who was getting operated on, my son's name, and would say, "I'm praying for your son and for the doctor today." I was so overwhelmed with emotion. My son was about to go through a life-or-death surgery, and yet I was so full of peace. The unexplainable, undeniable hand of God was at work there in that hospital that day. My baby came through the surgery successfully, and God gave me peace beyond understanding through it all.

They placed him in the critical care unit. He was the only child in there with several adult patients. The staff was amazing, but there was this one nurse that was so special. She would rock him in this rocking chair in the unit. She would take him around to visit the other patients, spreading some joy and smiles to them. Even at nine to ten weeks old, God began using him to bring joy to others' lives. Oh, how this melts a mama's heart!

CHAPTER 4

I DO, UNTIL ...

Once we got back home from my son's surgery, I went back to work. Money was getting much tighter, so I took a job in another county for more pay. It took both of our incomes to pay the monthly bills, and I was responsible for keeping up with that, which was brought on by myself.

My new job was centered around a satellite office for a real estate company. It was opened temporarily to see if this location would be profitable for the company. It seemed worth the risk of me leaving my current job to go to this location for a $10,000 annual salary increase plus benefits. It came with a longer commute, which took more time away from home. I was stressed enough over finances, and this didn't help, feeling like I was losing more time with my family.

Even with me taking this new job, the cost of living was harder to meet. I found myself growing bitter and resentful, feeling like I was carrying the stress and making the sacrifices alone. Isn't that how we feel when there is trouble in any relationship? We tend to blame each other rather than look at our part in the situation, whether it is financial or some other issue. And financial disagreements are effective in dividing and destroying relationships.

Generally, people are not taught how to budget. If they know how to complete a budget to see if they make more than they spend, they are not necessarily taught about cash flow, saving, or preparing for incidental or emergency expenses. It is an unfortunate crisis in our country because we have become accustomed to living paycheck to paycheck or spending first, worrying later. Had it not been for my mother sitting me down at age eighteen to teach me how to budget, I would not know how to manage personal finances either. She taught me how to budget, including all the expenses to factor in, such as gas, groceries, and emergencies. Her words of advice were, "If you don't have $500 left over at the end of every month, you will not live comfortably." That was the truest statement she ever made to me about money. There were periods of my life where I had that much at the end of the month, sometimes had more, and sometimes had less. But it served as a guidepost for me.

When a couple shares in financial obligations, there can be many conflicts that arise. For example, each one may have their own plans or ideas of how much to save versus how much to spend. Some disagree on how money should be spent. One may be more of a free spender while the other may be more frugal. One may work on commission or be self-employed with no assurance of a specific amount of income to rely on consistently. One may have to make a job or career change that requires a cut in pay. One may become unemployed for various reasons. Medical issues may arise, bringing financial hardship to the relationship.

Life is going to happen. But finances are not what actually destroy a relationship. The denial of the problem, lack of communication, lack of teamwork, and blaming each other is what causes the division between partners.

There may be plenty of solutions to financial problems, but we will never know if we can't first admit the problem exists. Let's assume we are able to admit the problem is there. It does us no good to admit it if we let things like pride stand in our way of seeking the advice of those with the solutions. Sometimes we are just not teachable, meaning we are not willing to learn how to navigate the issues because it requires too much effort or because we have a hard time taking advice from someone else. Are pride and ego worth holding on to at the cost of peace? Is it worth sacrificing your relationship?

Some people are just not willing to sacrifice for the team. There may be things either person could do, such as picking up extra hours or an extra job, selling some things that could cover the financial need, etc. When no action is taken, these issues tend to breed division. Division manifests in the form of blaming each other, attacking each other's character, and hurtful arguments. This division is a dangerous game to play because it is bait for one or both to seek comfort elsewhere. This comfort may come in the form of addictions, harmful habits, or in other people. It also may cause depression, anxiety, and a lack of faith, therefore affecting our spiritual relationship with God as well.

The point is, no matter the issue, communication and dedication are essential for the survival of a relationship. Being willing to grow and weather the storms of life together is key to the survival of the tough issues in any relationship.

Satan's plan of attack involves dividing the family unit any way he can, and he succeeded in mine once again because we let him. I became so consumed with what was happening around me that it led to more poor choices. After four years, with a two-year-old son, we divorced. It was very traumatic, one that would leave a wound for many years to come and brought on a great deal by my choices and decisions. When things got so bad and seemed unredeemable, I decided to fix an immediate issue that created long-term consequences once again, the only way I knew how, which was to close the door on it. But most of the time, you can't outrun your problems.

I noticed a pattern developing in my life. When times were tough, I would run to escape. That fight, flight, or freeze trauma response of the brain would kick in, and I would operate in flight mode. If a job was not going well or I felt stuck, I would leave it. If there was a struggle at home, I would leave it. I was always looking for peace everywhere but God. And for whatever reason, weathering a storm with God's help never crossed my mind. I loved God and wanted to live for God, but I didn't ever think to ask God what I needed to do. I always went in survival mode reactions.

I've learned a great deal about myself at this point in my life trying to heal old hurts and wounds. I have learned that I would go into flight mode to not ever feel trapped by someone like I felt as a kid. That trapped feeling of having to take the brunt of someone's anger and not being able to run left when I moved out on my own. And that relief was my reward.

CHAPTER 5

VALUE IN BOUNDARIES

Time to rebuild. I got hired for a customer service position at a large bank in the next town over. I sold my house to a couple that was looking for a larger home, and since they had a smaller home, I purchased their house. I can't explain what being able to own my own home without relying on anyone else to pay the bills did for me. It was the beginning of independence that I had never experienced in my twenty-eight years of life. No one could take it from me. No one could live there without my permission. No one could tell me what to do with it. No one could run me out of it. I could remodel if I wanted, paint if I wanted, and decorate it any way I wanted.

My home had a quaint cottage feel to it on the inside. It was 1,098 square feet with a one-car garage on an acre lot. There were two shade trees in the backyard beside a large wooden deck. My parents bought a swing set for my son, which fit perfectly in between the two trees. I bought him a green turtle sandbox and put it in the back under one of the trees. He loved playing in it too. We made that house a home, and we loved living there. It was the place where we had so little, but we had so much love. We baked cookies together, made picnics in the middle of the living room floor, and watched his favorite shows usually while sharing a big plate of fried okra. Surprisingly, it was one of his favorite foods. He had some little garden gloves, kid's bug scissors, and his little red wagon that we used when we trimmed the shrubs and flowers around the house. We hauled the clippings to the back of the lot to dump the clippings out of the wagon. We spent a lot of time there together just bonding over so many things. We were so poor, but so rich at the same time.

Even in the midst of bonding with my son, I hated myself so much. I hated that he now lived in a split home. I hated what I had become in the eyes of everyone around me. I hated that my family was now torn apart. I could barely stand to be in my own skin.

I began changing my lifestyle and habits to fit in with whoever I hung around and to numb the pain and anxiety I felt. People I believed to be my friends weren't. So much gossip and rumors, some true, some not true. It seems when people need encouragement and prayer the most, it is when others find pleasure in someone's pain and mistakes. It was a hurt and a bitterness that because I held on to them took me down worse roads. I don't blame anyone for anything. It was my choice. I could have dealt with the pain and ridicule differently. But I wasn't emotionally able to navigate through it at that moment, always reacting to situations in a trauma-brain response.

When I began dating again, I dated some guys who treated me well and some who did not. But it seemed the only ones I wanted to honestly date were the ones that treated me not so good. In some way, it was what I believed I deserved, therefore a level of gratification came with it as a form of self-punishment. I was addicted to a certain amount of chaos in my life at this point because it was becoming a way of life for me that was becoming comfortable. I didn't understand my addiction to chaos then, but in recovery, I learned that chaos would consume my mind and emotions at the moment, which was a distraction from the self-bashing thoughts in my mind. Times of peace gave me too much opportunity to dwell on the past, my mistakes, and what I would have done differently. Peace was not an option because there were too many unhealed wounds. So I chased enough chaos as a need for distraction.

The chaos at times came from abusive relationships. Whether verbal, mental, emotional, or physical, this abuse built fear and self-doubt so deep that I felt like I couldn't get out. When physical abuse occurred, it was only then that I longed for help to get out. I felt isolated and trapped and consumed alcohol to cope with it. I spent time coping by painting my house. I painted a lot, sometimes all night, to keep my mind occupied.

At this time, I was in an abusive relationship and had been in it for nearly a year. I was so far away from God that I felt like I couldn't pray for help to find a way out. Then one night, I had a dream that was so real, unlike any dream I had ever experienced to this point. In the dream, I was back at my parents' church where I grew up. I was kneeling on the floor in the center aisle, even with the first row of pews. I was facing the pulpit and the altar because I couldn't even make it all the way up to the altar. My son was lying across my lap. He was cold, stiff, and blue in color with wrinkled skin. His body was so heavy and getting colder. He had stopped breathing. In the dream, all the older members were there who used to attend when I was a child. They were standing in their pews facing the pulpit but turning their heads, looking down at me in disgrace. I was crying and screaming out for someone to help, someone to call 911, but they all just sat there looking at me. They never spoke, but their eyes said, "This is up to you. You are here because of your choices. It is your choice to help your son or not. We can't do it for you." I felt completely helpless to save my son, almost like he was being taken from me for reasons I had caused. Then as I woke up, it was as if I could hear a warning saying, "This is what you can expect if you don't get out of this place you are in." I felt tears running down my face. It was the first time I had ever physically cried while in a dream. I was so disturbed that I had to get up out of my bed and go lie across my son's little twin bed in his room since he was with his dad that night. I cried out to God so hard kneeling on the floor beside the bed. I told God how sorry I was for everything, and if He would give me strength and courage, I would get out of this place I had created in my life. It was one thing to battle over your child in a divorce, but this time, I was battling God, and I knew who would win that battle. God knew I needed this dream in so many ways. He knew the exact motivation it would take to face my fears and change my life and my relationship with Him.

I began to face my giants. I faced the fear of the unknown, and the days ahead were definitely going to be unknown. I faced temptations one minute and threats the next. The temptations were to slide back into the life I was pulling away from, and the threats came from those that did not want me to grow out of this place I had been.

When I made the decision to turn my life around, even the smallest boundaries I established were put to the test. I've learned that many people have a misconception about boundaries. I always thought a boundary was something you placed around others such as limitations, restrictions, or demands on someone in an effort to control the situation and ultimately the outcome. The problem with setting boundaries around someone else is that we are not their masters. We should not control another adult in such a way. Right or wrong, they are still an adult. To try to cage a person or force them into this "box" of limitations you created does nothing but choke out any hopes of growth for you or them. Boundaries are like the fence you build around *your* "house." It's the barrier that reflects what you will and will not allow in or near your own space. Boundaries are what you set around yourself, not others.

When you establish a boundary, do you have a hard time maintaining it? Let's look at why that might be. First, a boundary should be clearly thought out and, when necessary, communicated to others. Taking some time to decide what you want or don't want in your life is important. When it involves others, communicating your boundary up front lays a foundation for an understanding between you and them.

Secondly, decide how you will handle a situation when your boundary is pressed upon or violated. It is important to not attach a consequence with which you may not be ready to follow through. When you establish a boundary and then allow someone to compromise it, they then place as much value on it as you do. If you compromise it, it must mean they can too. We teach people how to treat us by the way we treat ourselves.

Since boundaries protect things of value, it is important to know what you value. Often, people assume all values are good. Values, however, are not automatically good things. People may value things that are not exactly healthy or create peace in their lives. For example, you may value power, money, and recognition to the point it creates hurt to those around you just to obtain it or protect it. Doing so may cause you to possess less of the fruits of the Holy Spirit found in Galatians 5:22–23. Does chasing after money cause you to be less kind when it comes to helping your fellow man? Does it rob you of the joy of family time because you are obsessively dedicated to a career that has taken top priority in your life all for the wealth it generates? Are you filled with jealousy by the successes or recognition of others? These are just a few examples of how what we truly value may be harmful.

There is an exercise I often have my coaching clients do. From a list of many different values, I have them spend some time examining a list of values and rating their top five values. This doesn't mean that they don't value more than these five things. It is only identifying the five most important things to them. I have found that a person's top five values are the things they protect the most; and when those values are violated by others, they find themselves dealing with anger, hurt, resentment, etc.

If you would like to do this exercise, simply spend some time examining different potential values. If you do not find a value that is important to you, feel free to create your own. First, narrow down to your top five most important values.

Next, think about different situations with which you feel some type of unresolved emotion that the situation may have created. This emotion is often anger for many people. How many of your top five values did the situation compromise?

Lastly, on a scale of 1–5 with 1 being the least and 5 being the most, rate your hurt, anger, and resentment you feel from this situation. Most people find that if they are angry on a level of 3, three of their top five values were violated and so on.

So what does this all mean? Knowing your values helps you clearly identify what is important to you. It helps you decide where to establish boundaries in your life in order to protect those values you hold dear. It may also explain to you why you feel so hurt or angry about a situation you may have been struggling to overcome. This exercise has helped many of my coaching clients understand their anger for the first time to begin tearing it down.

It is further important to understand that just because something is of value to you does not mean others will possess the same values. They may have another set of values they hold dear. And that is OK. This is where mutual respect is important in relationships. They may not even realize they have violated something important to you, and furthermore, having done so accidentally while upholding their own values. Learning how your values as well as the other person's values played a role in any anger or resentment may help you find empathy and understanding, leading to forgiveness and peace with the situation and those involved in it.

It is so easy to compromise boundaries and values in relationships. "But he said he will never do it again," you may have heard. Or, "She said she loves me even though she did this." A broken heart wants to believe these things, just like those in codependence would rather have a love that hurts than no love at all, just to not be alone. The thought of having boundaries is not even an option when reacting to situations out of fear of abandonment or fear of not being good enough. When fear of losing someone is the driving force in a relationship, self-worth takes a back seat for many people. It is important to get to know someone well, witnessing their walk rather than their talk. Does their talk match their walk? When you witness who someone is when you are not around, it's a truer picture of who they can be with you. It doesn't come with a need to impress you or manipulate you to gain your trust or love or to even possibly gain control of you. Taking the time to learn someone well before committing can save you a lot of hurt if you respect each other's values in the process.

The most important relationship you will ever have is a relationship with God. The love of God reminds you of who you are in His eyes when you have experienced hurt or disappointment. A relationship with God also keeps you from feeling alone if you invite Him into the many areas of your life. Nurturing that relationship on a regular basis to grow closer to God is a strength in the tough times and peace in the storms so that you can respond with wisdom rather than react to situations out of fear.

CHAPTER 6

KNOWING YOUR FATHER

Earlier, we learned that expectations can set the stage for disappointment. But what about God? Can't we expect Him to do what He says He will do? Absolutely, for God cannot lie (Titus 1:2 NAS95). So why doesn't God always answer your prayers? I'm here to tell you that He always answers our prayers. Sometimes the answer is the fact that He didn't answer. Sometimes the answer is no. Just because the Bible teaches us that God will do everything *He* says *He* will do does not equate to doing everything *we* ask Him to do. This is another twisted way Satan has brought confusion to the minds of believers who had enough faith to ask God for help through prayer and then leave them disappointed, resentful, and unbelieving when God doesn't answer the way they may have wanted.

God knows what is best for us. He knows what awaits around the corner that we cannot see. Sometimes we ask Him to answer our request in a particular way that we want Him to in a way that we think is best. His Word tells us in Isaiah 55:8 (NAS95), "'For My thoughts are not your thoughts, Nor are your ways My ways,' declares the LORD."

God sees everything everywhere, both the good and the bad (Proverbs 15:3). When He gives His answer to your prayers, whether the request is granted, denied, or modified, rest assured it is because He knows things you don't know. He sees things you can't see. You can probably identify a time in your life when you prayed for something specific and God didn't answer the way you asked Him to. You may have felt disappointed. Did you lose faith to any degree? Did you question God's existence or concern? If you found yourself blaming God, are you still blaming Him now? As you look back at where your life was then and where your life is now, you may identify that unanswered prayer as a blessing in disguise.

When we share with others an experience of disappointment, resentment, or disbelief we have had with God, we often hear them say, "Maybe there was a reason," to the point it has become cliché and, frankly, just fuels our anger about the situation. The truth of the matter is, there *was* a reason. We may never see the reason because we are too consumed with not getting what we wanted. For example, one morning, I was getting ready to leave my house for work. It had been raining extremely hard for hours the night before and early that morning. When I went to the door, I noticed the rain had run into my house around the door, soaking a considerable amount of floor space. Those floors had just been laid too. I tried to get up what I could and put towels down because it was still raining, and I had to get to work. This job was new to me, and I didn't want to be late being the new kid on the block. Needless to say, I left the house and drove fast to make up for the lost time.

I turned off of one highway onto the next, which has many curves and creeks running alongside the highway. As I was racing down the hill, rain covering the road and still pouring down, I saw that the creek's banks were overflowing and raging alongside the highway. There were places along the highway that had no guardrails. Anyone could hydroplane in this weather and easily end up in this raging creek. While driving, a feeling came over me that I can't explain even to this day. Somehow, I knew I was going to wreck that morning. It just swept over me, and an anxious panicking feeling came with it. I envisioned my vehicle flipped upside down in the creek with me in it. The thought alone was taking my breath away. Probably not even a half mile down the road, I saw a state trooper's lights come on as he pulled out behind me. It seemed like he came out of nowhere.

As the officer, there is no way I would have wanted to get out in that hard rain to issue someone a ticket. I was driving fourteen miles over the speed limit. All I knew at that moment was that he just saved my life. This trooper just literally saved my life today. I wasn't angry about being stopped or receiving a speeding ticket. Obviously, I was speeding. And now I would be even later arriving to work. I wasn't worried about how much the ticket would cost, the time it would take to have to go to court, driving school, or anything else. I could not have been more grateful to see that officer that day. I have never been grateful for a traffic citation, but I could have literally framed this one. I thanked God for using that officer and intervening, even if it was an inconvenience. It kept me alive. It kept me and possibly others injury-free. God could see what was around the corner that I couldn't see.

I also believe that God allowed me to *feel* the wreck about to happen and that my life was in danger because He used it to teach me something. No, the message was not about driving slower, especially in the rain. The message was, "See? This is how I watch after my children, even if it's inconvenient for them. I see what you cannot see. I know what you do not know. Trust me." This incident was such a spiritual-growth moment for me, trusting God all the more that He is in fact watching over me and taking care of me. It was a moment to build my trust in Him, that even when I'm not asking, He knows what I need. His Word tells us that He knows what we need even before we ask (Matthew 6:8 NAS95), and this just proved it to me in my own personal example.

Looking over your life, can you reflect for a moment about a time something didn't go your way? It may have been a time you prayed for intervention or maybe you hadn't thought to pray or even had time to pray at that moment. As you reflect on the outcome of the situation, did it work out in a way that was in your best interest, whether it was what you wanted or not? I hope this reflection increases your trust and faith in God to watch over your best interests too. Sometimes just reflecting on moments like this reminds us how much we are loved by our Creator. It helps us to see we are valued and that we matter to God, our Heavenly Father. We want God to protect us, and sometimes we become angry at Him when He does because the one He may be protecting us from is ourselves.

So if God is going to answer His way, why ask Him for anything? There are several reasons. One reason is that it gives Him a platform to grow your faith when you see how He answers your specific requests. Secondly, it's an act of humbleness when You can admit you need help. Thirdly, it's a display of inviting God into your life.

This is all part of growing a relationship of trust with God. God is not a genie in a bottle who exists to grant our requests. He is our Heavenly Father who wants a relationship with His children. A relationship consists of two-way communication. He wants to hear from us. He also wants us to give Him the time and space to respond and draw closer to Him to hear Him when He does. Whether it's that still small voice in your heart, signs, visions, dreams, or using other people or situations to speak to you, He wants to grow closer to you too.

When you ask God for something and He grants your request, it should build your faith. When you ask God for something and He does something different that worked out better for you, that should build trust with you. Faith and trust are different, yet both are necessary to have in your relationship with God.

Would you want to be in a relationship with someone that never spent much time with you? Is it even possible to form a true relationship with someone you never talk to? What if that person is always talking to you but never allows you time to talk back because of their busy lives or thoughtlessness? I don't know of any relationship that evolves without time and communication.

If you do all the speaking when you pray and never stop

to be still in His presence, you may be keeping Him from speaking to you in that still small voice. It may not be that God isn't trying to give you the answers or direction you seek. It may simply be a matter of not listening closely to hear Him. Invite Him to come and sit with you awhile so that you can begin to build your personal relationship with Him. He is not just in the soul-saving business or the business of granting help. He is not a lightning-bolt kind of God that is just waiting for you to get out of line to strike you down. He wants a relationship with you: all of you! And not just any relationship, but the kind of relationship a Heavenly Father has with you as His precious child.

As parents, we long for our children to come to us with their problems. We want them to seek advice from us, allowing us to be a part of their lives, especially in those teenage years when many kids tend to shut parents out more. Oh, how we long to nurture them and comfort them. We want to guide them and lead them, helping them to grow and mature into adulthood. I often wonder if God feels like we treat Him the way our teenagers treat us—only wanting to involve Him when we have to. We, much like our teenagers, often think we know what's best and don't want anyone telling us what to do. Even as adults, we often do this to our Heavenly Father. Yet just as teenagers when we are struggling, hurting, don't get our way, or in a crisis, who do we cry out for? Our Heavenly Father.

Maybe you are not a parent. Maybe you have great parents that are always there for you and have provided help, encouragement, and support throughout your life. How much greater your Heavenly Father wants to do the same! Matthew 6:26–30 (NAS95) explains just how great the depths of the Father's love is for you:

> Look at the birds of the air, that they do not sow, nor reap nor gather into barns, and yet your heavenly Father feeds them. Are you not worth much more than they? And who of you by being worried can add a single hour to his life? And why are you worried about clothing? Observe how the lilies of the field grow; they do not toil nor do they spin, yet I say to you that not even Solomon in all his glory clothed himself like one of these. But if God so clothes the grass of the field, which is alive today and tomorrow is thrown into the furnace, will He not much more clothe you? You of little faith!

You may not have had parents that showed love and care, but rather experienced situations of abuse and neglect, whether physical or emotional. Your first impression as a child of what God must be like often comes from the example your earthly father was to you. If your earthly father was a dictator, you may assume God must be. If your earthly father was an abuser, you may see Jesus as another man who doesn't care for you. This is an important insight for two reasons. First, fathers need to understand that the example you show to your children may help or hinder their relationship with God. Secondly, it is important to build a relationship with God to learn who He really is despite what you may have been shown by your earthly father. Maybe your father was absent from your life. You may have a hard time drawing close to God and feel like your relationship with Him is quite distant and hard to bond with.

We have all experienced a time where we have had thoughts and opinions about people we don't really know. And there is a good chance we have all been upset because someone had ideas or opinions of us that just were not accurate. They may never have bothered to get to know us before they made those determinations. Yet we do this to God when we choose to not know Him fully and yet form an opinion about Him that may not be accurate.

The more of the Word of God you study, the more you will learn about Him. The more you talk to God and allow Him the opportunity to speak back to you, the more you will grow a relationship with Him. The more you communicate with Him, the more you learn the sound of His voice to you. It is truly an amazing feeling when you can call on Him at any moment for any reason and feel heard, loved, and comforted.

CHAPTER 7

ORIGINS OF HURT

I want to take this moment to address those that have been victims of abuse. If you have been a victim of abuse, you may be wondering where was God when these things were happening to you. You may believe there is no justice with God because He didn't stop this person from hurting you.

Both good and evil exist in this world. The Bible teaches us in 1 Peter 5:8 (NAS95), "Be of sober spirit, be on the alert. Your adversary, the devil, prowls around like a roaring lion, seeking someone to devour." Satan wants to take down as many people as possible, and when he finds someone to devour, putting evil acts and thoughts into their minds, he sways them to act out these thoughts onto others, trying to devour others who are innocent victims in the situation. God didn't do this to you. Your abuser did, whether it was from their own character or whether they were under the influence of the evil in this world.

If you were hurt by others as a child, you had your own angel who *continually* saw the face of God. A warning from Jesus went out in Matthew 18:10 (NAS95) to those that might do evil to children, and it says this: "See that you do not despise one of these little ones, for I say to you that their angels in heaven continually see the face of My Father who is in heaven." I can just imagine the reports your angel was giving to God when you were hurting.

God wants you to give the pain and hurt to Him. It's okay to tell God how angry you are. It's okay to even tell God how you cannot seem to forgive the person who hurt you. Sometimes it may take going through some trauma work along with some spiritual work to heal the wounds. But unforgiveness is something God wants you to give to Him. It will hold on to you as long as you hold on to it. Just because someone tells you that you need to forgive others does not mean you can just decide to do so. It takes work to get to a place of healing so that you *can* forgive. I have, however, witnessed unforgiveness take everything from people who just would not forgive, much like a drug of choice isn't satisfied until it takes everything from someone in active addiction.

People tend to withhold forgiveness for many reasons, one being because it feels like doing so somehow allows this person to go free. Forgiveness is actually for you though, not to make them feel better. You are actually the prisoner to unforgiveness, yet refusing to forgive them in our minds makes us think we are holding them as a prisoner, freezing them in the act.

People who have been harmed will oftentimes hurt others in the way they were harmed. Sometimes it comes in the form of hurting the one who hurt you. Sometimes it gets projected on to innocent people around us. For example, when I was mad at my dad for not allowing me to go somewhere or do something my friends were allowed to do, I would often take it out on my mom. And she had nothing to do with it. She would not override his rules and decisions out of respect. So I would get mad at her because if I talked back to my dad, there were consequences. But Mom just loved me through it. I will forever regret the times my words and attitude hurt her. She did not deserve it whatsoever.

The person who hurt you is no different. You may or may not know the person very well that hurt you. If you do, you may be able to identify where their hurt comes from, which may help you understand the "why" they may have hurt you. This by no means excuses or diminishes the impact it had on you. It does not give them a free pass or excuse for hurting you or anyone else either. But sometimes the beginning of forgiveness begins when you are able to understand why it happened.

If your abuser ever shared the hurts they have experienced throughout their lives, you may find similarities in the pain they felt and the pain they caused you. If there are patterns of abuse, it usually has nothing to do with you not being good enough or flawed in some way to them. It may just be a pattern of behavior they have developed out of past traumas in their own lives.

Forgiving someone also does not mean you have to reconnect with them. It is not always safe to encounter them, especially if they have not worked on healing themselves. Sometimes it helps to write a letter to the person saying what you wish you could say or journal about the hurt just as a means of releasing it, even if it is on paper that you never do anything with. There again, the forgiveness is not for their benefit. It is for yours so that you can heal and be set free of the hardness it may have caused in your heart.

God healed me and set me free of the unforgiveness I felt because of abuse in bad relationships. It wasn't until I found empathy for them by seeing how they had been hurt and how their hurt played a part in the hurt I experienced.

I pray this prayer for you, and if you can honestly pray with me in agreement (Matthew 18:19 NAS95), I believe God will hear and He will answer by beginning to lead you through the process of breaking the chains that have held on to you:

> Father, I pray for those victims of abuse that are reading this right now. I pray that you will let them feel in their heart the love you have for them. I pray that you will let them know just how much you hurt when you saw them being hurt. I pray that you will assure them that you are the God who heals and sets free those trapped in the clutches of pain and abuse. Please create a willingness in them to heal, to open up to You and to someone who can guide them through any trauma they may have experienced while including You in the process. I pray You will begin even now to loosen and break the chains the abuse has held on them and their lives. Remind them, Lord, of the love You have for them and, if they will let You, that You want

so much to have a relationship with them, to know their hurt and their pain, and are ready to lead them to freedom. In your Son, Jesus's name, I pray these things. Amen.

CHAPTER 8

NEW LIFE, NEW PEOPLE, NEW ACTIONS

After my third divorce from a quick marriage that only lasted a couple of years and had much of my unhealed baggage in the middle of it, I was quickly swept away by my codependent tendencies. It was a new year, new life, and new people. I was introduced to social media at that time. It was exciting reconnecting with friends I had not seen in many years. With that came some not-so-welcomed contacts. I began to get private messages that I wanted no part of and furthermore made me lose a great deal of self-esteem. I began to question myself as to what must they think of me to think I would engage with them. Then I began to look at myself, to examine what image I was portraying. Although necessary, that self-examination caused me to relive the choices and decisions that brought me to this place of truth: My actions over the last five years were not exactly Christlike. I was at the all-time lowest point of my life, feeling worthless and like a failure. I felt as though I had ruined my son's life most of all, no matter how much I tried to make sure he felt as minimal effects of divorce as I knew how, and now he was having to go through it again. I was even fearful when he went to school, afraid some parents wouldn't allow their child to be friends with him because of the example I had been.

The more I was approached and treated like an object that had no emotion, felt no pain, and had no conscience, the more I believed those things to a degree. I was on a freight train going downhill that just lost its brakes. I was hanging out with friends I love dearly that I partied with at our homes in the quiet. I dated people without asking any questions. Some were in the middle of divorces, which I was unaware because I never stopped to ask questions. Some had an unhealthy relationship with drugs, alcohol, control, etc. It didn't matter to me though. I was craving the attention to feel lovable because I certainly did not love myself. I had very few boundaries when it came to myself, therefore going along with many things that violated values I used to hold dear to my heart.

This year, I coped with my life in unhealthy ways. As long as I had my son with me, I was great. When he was away with his dad, I struggled to be by myself. I wanted to change. I wanted to be different. I wanted to be someone people could look at and say, "Now, that's a good woman right there." I wanted to be a person who could express her faith in God and help others understand Him as I thought I did. And the more I wanted it, the more I realized how far away I was from it. The thought in my mind that kept saying, "You will never be that, you are too far gone," was building hopelessness within me so deep that I was losing the strength to fight.

I started having anorexic behaviors again, which I had not done in years. My hair was falling out from starvation. People would tell me how bad I looked, that my eyes were sunken and I needed to eat. But it seemed to be the only way I could have some control in my life over how I felt about myself. The smaller I got, the better I felt about myself. It was the only thing I had left. If I couldn't feel good about myself on the inside, I certainly could control if I felt good enough about myself on the outside, however damaging and toxic it was.

One morning, I slept in a bit longer because I was taking off work for a doctor's appointment later that day. My bedroom in my house had two windows, both with the blinds closed. I always closed my blinds at night right before it got dark outside. When I woke up that morning, the minute my eyes opened, there was a brightness I can't explain. The glow in my room coming through those windows was abnormally bright. I questioned if I forgot to close the blinds, but no, they were closed. The whole room seemed to be illuminated like a glowing sunbeam that filled the entire room. I felt this comforting peace wrapping around me, which I had never felt this feeling before. It was like being in the presence of angels, only none were visible. As I lay there for a few moments trying to wrap my mind around what was happening, I heard God speak to me for the second time maybe in my life in this direct way. Sure, I felt promptings from the Holy Spirit before to maybe testify in church on occasion or to go speak to someone, but this was completely different. It was a fatherlike voice that wasn't audible, yet I could hear it plainly. The words were, "It is finished. This five-year self-punishment is over. Now clean out your house. I have something coming." I raised myself out of my bed in complete awe and disbelief! What just happened? What literally just happened?

I needed no explanation to know that "my house" meant my life and its current state. At that moment, I felt the purest love I've ever felt since the day I was saved by His grace. Tears were running down my face and joy running through my veins. Could it be? Could it really be that I matter enough to God that He just sent a message to me? And not just a message, but He was also planning to do something in my life just for me? Oh, how unworthy, how undeserving I felt. Feeling completely humble at that moment, it was as if I wasn't what others said or thought of me. I wasn't what I personally thought of myself. Hope came rushing over me! Could I honestly be able to be forgiven and really be healed of the pain of my failures? This whole experience felt like how the woman at the well must have felt the day she encountered Jesus. I related to her so much in this moment. But she was actually in a face-to-face conversation with Jesus. I can't imagine how that must have felt. He might not have been in my room in the flesh that morning, but I heard that still small voice speaking to me.

This feeling stayed with me, and so did those words. God spoke to me that day with something so concrete and definitive that I had no doubt whatsoever that something was about to happen. As my day went on and the days ahead, I almost caught myself looking in anticipation around the corners everywhere I went, looking for this "something good." What was it going to be? Or who was it going to be?

I began cleaning out my house, praying for forgiveness from old and new sins, and praying to be drawn close to God so that I didn't miss anything, especially His voice. I began hanging out with some really good friends that just kind of morphed into a small little tribe. We were always there for each other. We went places and did things together just enjoying each other's company with no strings attached. I needed this while I was cleaning out my house so to speak, not filling it up with anyone new to engage in a relationship with. I was trying to draw closer to God, listening and waiting.

As part of this "cleaning out" process, I made myself sit at home one evening while my son was gone at his grandmother's house. I needed to learn how to be alone without occupying myself with conversations by text, phone calls, or social media. I needed to learn how to just *be* in my own home alone and experience peace. One night, I decided I was going to stay home alone and search for that peace. I made myself stay off my phone as much as possible, not going anywhere with friends, and just trying to sit alone with myself. As I sat in my recliner rocking while watching TV, I became restless, wanting to grab my phone and try to engage in any conversation I could with my friends. I was so tempted to see if some of my friends wanted to hang out. But I pushed through the urges. As I sat there and rocked back and forth while watching TV and growing more restless, I knew if I was going to successfully do this, I needed Jesus. I then uttered one request to Jesus, "Jesus, will you just come and sit with me awhile?"

What happened next was so surreal. Across from me was

my loveseat. I felt peace coming from that side of the room. It was so warm and comforting. I remember saying, "You are here, aren't you? I feel your presence." The restlessness I had been feeling was calming inside as the warmth in the room was growing. That room became so soothing that I didn't even want to go to the kitchen to get something to eat for fear it would not feel the same when I returned.

"God, if you are here with me, please go into the kitchen with me while I get something to eat," I remember praying. I got up, went into the kitchen, and felt that same warmth follow me there. This was one of the most amazing things I had ever experienced up to this point. By the time the night was over, no matter where I went in my house, I felt that peace everywhere. That night, my house became a home. It became the place I wanted to run to, not run away from. It became my haven. I couldn't wait to get there after work each day and be alone there even just to soak up the peace that was inside of it now.

Some time passed, and one evening, two of my friends were over visiting. We were sitting on my front porch, and one of them received a phone call from a friend of theirs whom I had never met. As they talked, he just handed me the phone and asked me to talk to this person. I had no idea who was on the other end of the line.

"Hello?" I said.

The voice on the other end said, "Hello?"

I asked, "Who is this?"

The voice then asked, "Who is this?"

Not knowing what to say to each other, we were both intrigued it seemed with what little we did speak. I handed the phone back to my friend and didn't put much more thought into it.

One evening, some of our friend tribe decided to go eat for dinner. I opted not to go because I had my son and was spending time with him. So they rode out to my house to visit a few minutes before leaving. The unidentified caller happened to be with them. Now I had a name and a face and a personality. His name was Adam. He was tall and handsome, had beautiful eyes, and a beautiful smile. He seemed happy and just an all-around good guy. They ended up staying awhile, and I was glad I got to meet Adam, my new friend.

How I have lived in this small town for ten years never running into him, never meeting him, I will never know. Now, all of a sudden, I was seeing him everywhere it seemed. Standing in line with my son at a restaurant inside one of our stores in town, I saw him coming into the store. He saw me too, which is not an area of the store people usually notice from my experience. We waved at each other, spoke for a few moments, and went on our way.

The next encounter was when the bank where I worked had an annual training an hour away in the evening for all employees to be able to attend. Our branch employees all went together to the training. When we arrived back at our branch later that night, we all filed out of the vehicle we rode in to the meeting. As I was standing in the parking lot talking with one of my coworkers, I got a message that said, "I see you."

I didn't recognize the number and replied, "Who is this, and where are you?" I was looking all around and didn't notice anything unusual. I got a reply: "Look behind you." I turned around, and there was a black truck getting money out of the ATM at another bank that had a parking lot across the road from our bank parking lot. It was Adam! He drove over to us, made some small talk, then asked if we wanted to go ride around with him for a bit. My coworker and I accepted the offer; and we laughed, talked, and had a great time.

One evening later, Adam and one of our mutual friends rode out to my house to visit. They weren't there long; and right before they left, Adam came back in, walked over to me and kissed me, then left. Wow! I was standing there in my living room in shock and awe over what just happened. It was such a pure and innocent moment. It was a moment when I felt as though someone saw me, the real me, not as an object, but as a treasure. He expected nothing from me, nor was he trying to use this moment to lead to something more. He just kissed me and left. It was so innocent and sweet. My heart was melting. A few days later, I got a message from him asking if I wanted to go riding again. I was excited and quickly said, "Yes!" This time, it was just him and I, which made it easier to learn more about each other.

Being from a small town with nowhere to really hang out, people usually went riding around on country roads for fun. At that time, social media wasn't dominating people's lives so much, so we actually spent more time together talking in person and getting to know one another. At this point, I began wondering, "God, is this what the 'something good coming' is about? Is it Adam?"

Before meeting Adam, I had grown so tired of relationships

that kept ending, relationships that kept hurting. I was at work one day sharing with an old friend who came by the woes of my past relationship and how I was in this state of hopelessness. You know you have a real friend when he or she will tell you the truth even when it hurts. After listening to me, he made the most profound statement to me: "You do realize you are the common denominator in each relationship, right?" That comment pierced me to the core. I wasn't angry at all, but it was a moment of truth, and finally someone cared enough about me to point out that I needed to change. I took it to heart and really tried to do some self-examination. Why did I fall for someone so fast? Why, when I knew I probably didn't need to be with that person, did I entertain the relationship anyway? I began looking at other couples I felt were successful in making their relationships work. What were they doing differently? One thing was that I fell in love first and asked questions later, if at all. I just took whatever from whomever in order to feel loved and accepted. But it seemed that I only wanted relationships with those that were difficult to keep. If someone loved me easily, I didn't want it. It wasn't challenging enough. Why was that? What was wrong with me? Would I ever be able to have a comfortable, easy relationship with someone? I didn't understand why I was the way I was, but I knew I had to change something if I could ever expect to get a different result.

The next time Adam and I hung out, he came to my house to pick me up for a date. After much reflection over my life and my normal habits, I made up my mind that while I could still think with my mind, I was going to handle this very differently. When he came to pick me up, we were standing in my kitchen. We began discussing where we thought this might go. That's when I mustered up all the courage I had in me. Inside, it felt like I was taking deep rapid breaths just before stepping into a boxing ring about to fight a giant. After all, I was about to face my giant: I was about to set boundaries at the risk of someone walking away and abandoning me for doing so.

With the fear of what might happen next and just an ounce of courage, I said to Adam, "I'm about to tell you where I've been in my life, where I'm at, and where I'm going, and if there is any part of it that you don't like, there is the door. You can see your way out because right now, I'm still able to think with my head. And I know me. Before long, I won't be able to think with my head, but only with my heart. And I *will not* go through this again. I'd rather be alone. I'm not doing this to my son again."

Wow! That felt so good. It felt so empowering. I could actually take control of my emotions and set boundaries for myself and who I wanted to be. I could own my past and claim my future at the same time! And all it took was God, courage, and a willingness to change, to do something different. That had to be God's power taking over in my weakness because I had never been strong enough to do that before. I had been conditioned from childhood that to speak up or share what was on my mind equaled punishment, anger, and undesirable consequences. I know now that's why I never could feel empowered in relationships. I was trained that having a voice was unacceptable until I found mine.

From there, we talked for the next three hours about our

lives, down to details of how we had been raised, what we believed in spiritually, our hurts in our life, and our plans for our futures. It was the most open and honest conversation I think I've ever had with someone I could possibly find myself in a relationship with.

The Bible teaches about being equally yoked in a relationship. In the weeks and months ahead, I began learning what yoking looked like, and we established that we both believed in God. We had the desire to get our walks stronger with God and return to church attendance to grow spiritually.

Within weeks, we became exclusive. We were a couple, now off the market. He was not on social media, so I deleted my accounts too. I hadn't had those accounts long anyway. I wanted to build trust with him so much because he had experienced his own hurts in the past. For the record, he never asked me to do this. I found myself wanting to earn his trust. This may have been more for my own benefit than his now that I reflect on that. To find someone, anyone who seemed to truly love me maybe meant there was something still good left about me. I wanted to be the woman I always thought I would be growing up, but fell so short. It seemed that I may just have one more chance to turn my life around, and that was purely from God's unconditional love and grace. I quickly knew that this was what God woke me up to tell me that morning months ago. This was God's gift of grace.

CHAPTER 9

TRIALS TO FUEL FAITH

Adam and I became very dedicated to each other. He was everything I had ever wanted all wrapped up into one person: God-loving, kindhearted, provider, respected, strong, passionate man that may seem like a teddy bear but would protect and defend his family to the end. And did I mention he was very handsome? Yep, God did that. I know I believed there was no one out there that could possibly possess all those qualities together. But God doesn't do things halfway. So when God selected the one for me, He blessed me with all these amazing qualities I love so much about Adam.

Adam was growing close to my son, and my son was following him everywhere, loving Adam in his life. We were growing so close to each other, and both of us just knew we were what we had been praying for. We were engaged within five months and married two months later. Some people felt it was too quick. Some were thinking, "Here she goes again." But in my heart, I knew he was the one for me. I've been asked so many times, "How did you know?" My reply is always, "God gave him to me. This I know for a fact."

During those dating months, we established boundaries to build trust. We decided that we would go nowhere without the other one. If the world couldn't understand it, it didn't matter. It was what we believed was going to work for us, being as we had both been through hurts that caused trust issues. We took a great deal of criticism from friends for it and actually turned down things we would have liked doing with our friends when he or I couldn't tag along. After a while, it became our way of life. Our friends and family grew to expect it and eventually quit asking unless they were inviting us both. We had truly become best friends, actually enjoying spending so much time together.

We were done with the party scene. We couldn't wait to get home to each other in the afternoons. I would have dinner fixed. We would eat at the table with my son and play games sometimes afterward. We were becoming a real family, something I thought would never be possible with a split-family situation. Dinnertime alone was like a healing ointment to my old self-inflicted wounds. We were calm, peaceful, and never fought.

Oh, the honeymoon phase! It's such a deceiver at times, but great while it lasts. I believe it is God's way of getting you so in love with each other that you have some reserves built up for when things are less than perfect.

We developed this adventurous life together, from snow skiing to motorcycle riding, to driving on country roads to watch the sun go down, eating out frequently on dates with each other, and traveling. Our life was a dream come true: family stability, financial stability, adventure, and most importantly, a walk with God. It truly was a gift from God.

I had not experienced this kind of relationship with anyone in my life. We were blessed in ways I've never experienced all at one time.

Our jobs were going great. I went back to college, completing my degree in business management. I was moving up in my position at the bank I worked for at that time. Both Adam and my son were so supportive of my decision to further my education. They would help out around the house cooking, cleaning, and helping any way they could. Sound too good to be true? It wasn't. It was a blessing, which is what God gives you when you listen to Him. Make no mistake, a blessing doesn't mean perfect. We were far from perfect. It also doesn't mean you won't experience hardships, struggles, or challenges. I've always heard the saying, "What goes up must come down." This was true for us, but not in the way you may think.

I had been in school for eight years at this point. People would ask me if I planned to continue, but I needed a break in a big way. Work had been supremely busy, and banking regulations were so extreme that it made my job very stressful. The consequences for not crossing a *t* or dotting an *i* could have potentially damaging effects including penalties and/or time served for breaking the law. I feared this so much because our compliance department was always sure to tell us all the worst of the worst things that could happen if we made costly errors. I literally had nightmares that regulators would pull up to the front door in black suits, black SUVs with tinted windows, and sunglasses—you know the look. They would walk in to question me about an error on a document or something that I had forgotten to do on a particular loan file. I lived with this fear for nearly ten years, and I literally prayed on a regular basis that God would help me catch my mistakes *before* I made them.

My prayer time was early in the morning, between 3:30–4:30 AM. It seemed that I could find God easiest during that time each morning before the sun came up and everything inside and outside was calm and peaceful. My bedroom became my prayer sanctuary when Adam would leave for work each day. I spent that hour or so with God, reading His Word, devotionals, and praying.

After graduating, I found myself for the first time in years sitting in a comfortable recliner each evening, playing a game on my phone, and watching TV. After about a month of this, I began thinking and praying, "Is this all there is? Is this all there is left to life? Just coming home and doing this? There are people dying and going to hell every day, and all I can do is sit here in this comfortable house, in this comfortable chair, playing a game, and watching something on TV that I shouldn't even be watching. God, if you will give me something to do for you and the courage to do it, I'll go." Word of warning: don't ask God for something to do if you aren't ready to act on it.

Shortly thereafter, one morning about midway through my prayers, God gave me a vision with instruction. It was a vision of a room in the county jail that had folding tables in it and chairs. I saw myself working with those ladies who were incarcerated. Then I heard, "All this time you have worried about making an error at work that would land you in jail when it was never that at all. I've been grooming you to go into the jail to work with the ladies. Now go and tell the person I have shown you who would help." *Wow!* Just ... *wow!* It was one of the most real visions and experiences I have ever had with the Lord up to this point. It was such a huge relief in a sense because at that very minute, my fear of jail began to leave me. It was uneasy at the same time because I was definitely out of my comfort zone and had no idea what to expect or where to even start. But as always, God worked that out too. This whole experience led me to volunteer at a recovery home for ladies for a year, doing Bible studies and music lessons.

During that year, there was a huge wedge driven between Adam and I. Volunteering at the recovery home was really the second thing we had ever done apart from one another in eight years. The only other thing we would do on occasion without the other was going on the Saturday motorcycle ride with the group of friends. If he had to work, I would sometimes go. If I had something to do or wasn't feeling up to it that day, he sometimes went without me. Other than that, we had never done anything really without the other and definitely not on a regular basis. He couldn't take part in this ministry with me much since this recovery home was only for ladies. It wasn't because I didn't want him there. I wanted nothing more than for us to serve together.

I immediately fell in love with this mission. It was so fulfilling to see these girls finding hope and joy, learning about God, and healing. I would come home so excited, only to find Adam so hurt and feeling forgotten. The more involved I became there, the harder things got at home for both of us. The more hurt he felt, the more hurt I felt. The more hurt I felt, the more I would put into this ministry, all in the name of God, of course, because after all, God said for me to do this, right? And that was even something he wouldn't deny. Adam would always say he knew God called me to this.

I had the hardest time understanding why this was all happening. I found myself staying at work later just to avoid conflict. Home had been my place of peace, but peace was nowhere to be found. Weary of the situation, I began to question God, "God, I know you told me to do this. I know it! But why would you call me to do something that was causing my marriage to suffer, which I know is not pleasing to you either? I don't understand. I also know you gave Adam to me. Why now would you ask something of me that was going to be so hard for us to accept? He feels like I have abandoned him. Set me free of this, please. I can't take this anymore. Why, God, why? I can't make Adam have passion for my purpose."

One evening, after returning from the ministry, as Adam lay on the couch, I sat on the floor in front of him in our living room. We were talking, but he wouldn't really look at me. I asked what was wrong, and he then said, "I don't know how much more of this I can take."

I took an emotional gut punch right there on the floor. "What do you mean? Are you leaving me?" I asked. At that moment, it was as if my whole world was crashing down. All he would say was that he didn't know how much more he could take, never clarifying what he meant by that.

As I sat on my knees on the floor beside him waiting for our fate to be decided, I bowed my head for a moment as I sat there in silence and told God, "I'll go with You, God. Just please take care of me and my son no matter what happens next." At that moment, a calmness ran through me. It was a peace I could not explain, yet my heart was breaking because I didn't want to lose Adam or our life together.

I looked up and calmly said words I can't believe ever came out of my mouth. "If you are asking me to choose between you and God, you won't like the outcome." It was at that moment, such a huge moment for both of us, that change occurred. I loved him so much and didn't want to lose him. I knew this was a test for me. I can't imagine what Abraham felt when he walked Isaac up to that mountain, but I know it took faith to trust God for intervention. And at this moment, I needed that same faith. I put all the faith I had into God, turning this around right then and there.

Almost instantly, Adam began to say that he wasn't going anywhere, and the doors of communication flung open. After talking more, God began changing things for both of us. It wasn't easy for several months, but I could see and feel progress. I had some changes to do, which I couldn't see up to this point. It felt like I had been wearing blinders to my part in all of it. I had put this ministry above Adam in the name of God when God never said for me to *worship* the ministry. He said for me to worship Him and serve my family and the ministry. The ministry was the platform to serve God and worship Him, not a gift God gave to me to worship in His place to the point I neglected my first platform to serve, which was my family. I caused this, not Adam. And the tension I had toward him for being upset and blaming him for what I caused was now all on me.

This was all such a test and a challenge for me because I

had been codependent all my life until God set me free of it when he woke me that morning in my room. He made me a promise that day of a gift, which happened to be Adam. The hours-long conversation Adam and I had in my kitchen when we began dating snapped the chains of codependence loose when I faced my fears of loneliness and abandonment. And this whole experience was another growth moment for us both, preparing us for a new level of sacrifice up ahead.

If this had all happened prior to those chains being snapped, I would have walked away from God's assignment for me, I very likely wouldn't be where I am today. My fear of being left and abandoned would have overshadowed my obedience to God's calling. Our next assignment would require even more of Adam and I both, and we would need greater faith to actually follow God's lead into the deep. This whole experience grew us both closer to each other and closer to God.

God tests our obedience to grow our faith. He also tests our stewardship of the blessings He gives us so that the blessings do not become our idols. He uses these tests as a platform to grow us to the next level. Unfortunately, that requires us to be in uncomfortable places, places that are challenging and hard. That's why these pains are called "growing pains." If we walk away from those platforms before giving God the opportunity or space to show us His power, we forfeit the development of deeper levels of faith, sanctification, and service in His Kingdom.

God didn't just pluck the Israelites out of Egypt and drop them into the promised land. He put them through trials and hardships to manifest His power, growing their belief in Him. He then began to chisel the "Egypt" off them so that they would love and serve Him. We cannot handle the great places God plans to take us without some grooming and preparation for those places. We would self-sabotage if He gave us a purpose or calling we didn't yet have the faith to handle or believe for it.

CHAPTER 10

WALKING IN PURPOSE

The next phase of service involved leaving my career and salary that sustained a good portion of our bills and lifestyle, to open a nonprofit coaching facility that helps those battling addiction, personal issues, and homelessness. When God led me to give up the career I loved more than anything I had ever done to enter ministry, I spent about five to six months arguing with God about it, trying to use every excuse I could find as a reason to change God's mind. But God didn't let up.

During this time, I could tell Adam's heart was softening. He was very supportive of this mission unlike anything I had ever imagined. When the construction began on the center and I felt God telling me to give up my fifteen-year career in the banking industry to volunteer full-time at the center, I never believed Adam would agree to it whatsoever. I held it in for a couple of months while praying, trying to make sure that I was truly hearing God's direction correctly because this was a life-altering decision. We would have to live off my retirement, and I believed I had enough in my retirement to sustain us for one year before it would be exhausted. I had no idea what would happen after that if I would go back to work or if God would do something miraculous.

One evening, I shared with Adam that I felt God drawing me away from the bank to give all I had to this mission for at least one year. Even though I had prayed up and given this moment to God multiple times over, I was still surprised at the response he gave. Adam said, "If God is telling you to do it, you have to do it. Right now, it will feel like we are fighting the devil, but if you don't do it, then we are fighting God, and we know who wins that one. I'm all for it." What just happened? Is this even real? God had completely changed his heart!

The whole exodus from the bank was another miraculous story in itself, but I will save that for another time. And everything that has happened since that decision has been like watching miracles happen that you only read about. I have been with this organization now for over three years. God has blessed us in miraculous ways, both our marriage and the organization. And one of the best parts was the morning Adam woke me up to say goodbye before going to work. I made a comment that he should just go to work with me today. He said, "My job is to make sure I work hard to keep you afloat to do the job God has called you to do. This I know." Could it be that he has been talking to God about his own purpose? He shared it with such profound certainty that my heart just melted. God took all that bitterness we felt from a few years ago and filled us with purpose and joy—and not just any purpose. He aligned our purposes so that we are working toward a common goal.

And so it was that we were equally yoked with the yoke God gave us. Let me explain what a yoke is for those who may not know. And no, we aren't talking eggs here. A yoke is a big plank of wood with two notches cut out in the bottom of it. It was placed onto the neck of two oxen to make them a team. It had reins that were held by the person guiding the team. When I began to study what the Bible says about being equally yoked, how the husband is part of the wife and the wife is part of the husband and how the two become one, I got a visual of what it would look like to be pulled in two different directions.

Imagine a team of oxen plowing a field. The ox on the right side looks to his right and thinks that row looks easier to plow. It begins to veer in that direction. A tug-of-war begins between the team. They aren't very productive at this point because they are torn between purpose and desire.

Imagine if the ox on the left was sluggish and unmotivated. This ox may not be motivated for the team's benefit, and the ox on the right feels like it is dragging its partner in a three-legged race until exhaustion makes carrying the weight of both too difficult to carry anymore. They are not marching together toward the same goal and therefore are struggling with unity.

Imagine the team of oxen having a common desire to support each other, but there is no guide holding the reins. This team wanders aimlessly toward whatever catches their eye at that time. If it sounds like a good idea to one, the other follows until they end up in rows they were not meant to plow in their lives.

Now, imagine this team yoked together for the same

purpose and support for each other, but that mission was not their own. It was God's plan for them in their lives and matches or complements each other's purpose. They work together, undivided and blessed because of the surrender to the Master's plan. They have peace.

Let me make something clear. This does not mean this team doesn't ever face hardships, trouble, or downfalls from time to time. Just like plowing a field, there are dips, holes, rocks, and often thorns to have to deal with. The point is that the team is not left alone to figure it out for themselves. They have a guide—*the* Guide if they allow God to lead. This Guide will be there when the dirt in the field is soft and smooth or filled with boulders. *He* will never leave you. For Adam and I, our guide finally became God. Oh, how things changed in our lives when He began to lead all aspects of our lives!

Where are you in your life? Are you equally yoked to the one God has for you, or are you trying to yoke to someone that is not meant to plow the same row God has prepared for you? If your gut is churning right now at the mere mention of this statement, then it may be a good time to self-examine why you are in this place of unrest. Have you earnestly asked God if you are with who you are meant to be? Many won't because they already deep down know the answer, and if they pray and ask God, He may just confirm that gut feeling. Then they are faced with making a tough decision either way: a decision to walk away or a decision to move forward out of God's will. If you have never honestly asked God for direction in your relationship, this would be a great place to start before you decide to marry the wrong person.

Maybe it's about a career choice for you. Are you torn about what career you are supposed to embrace? Or maybe it is about where you should live. This principle applies to all aspects of life. Will you allow God to hold the reins in all areas of your life?

For those who are married to someone already, and you feel like you both are not on the same page in life, have you communicated with each other about it? It is amazing what a simple conversation that involves a true desire to understand each other can do. I am talking about a conversation that aims to understand each other rather than being fixated on getting your way. In coaching couples, I find that so many people can't even talk to each other or open up about their hopes, dreams, and fears. Their differences and self-seeking desires often cloud their ability to hear each other and limit their willingness to compromise. But when they do, they find common ground to build upon, a ground they never knew existed between them.

My past mistakes can be attributed to three main things: not asking God first, not waiting on God to deliver, and not surrendering to God's direction. There is nothing like living in the purpose God gives you with the one God gives you. I know firsthand. I've tried it every other way possible. I had to beat codependence to get there, and that took the power of God over my will and my life to defeat. Codependence is a beast that is so toxic. It will destroy more than it will ever supply. It is not real love. It is a need to not feel lonely or abandoned. It is a need to be accepted or to belong and to feel like you are enough in someone else's eyes rather than God's eyes or even your own.

My prayer for you is that if you are identifying with what you have read here, you will seek to build the greatest relationship you'll ever build. A relationship with God will never be codependent. God doesn't operate in that manner. A relationship with God allows you to see yourself how the One who created you sees you: with love. A relationship is not one-sided either. Sometimes it requires you to be still and allow the other person to speak while you listen intently. Are you giving God the room to speak, and better yet, are you listening intently to what He may say? I encourage you to get to know Jesus Christ—our Savior, Healer, Helper, Refuge, and Guide. The peace of your future depends on it!

Printed in the United States
by Baker & Taylor Publisher Services